Periphery within Periphery

A Challenge towards an Integrated

Manipur

Ch. Rupachandra Singh

ANSHAH Anshah Publishing House

Rs. 495; US$ 24.75

ISBN: 978-81-8364-090-9

Published in 2013

Periphery within Periphery: A Challenge towards an Integrated Manipur

Published by:
ANSHAH PUBLISHING HOUSE
LG, Pankaj Central Market, I.P. Ext.,
Patparganj, Delhi-110092, Tel: 22235152, 9810522367
Br.Off. 4617/18, Ansari Road, Darya Ganj,
New Delhi-110002, Tel: 65946453

To

Ech'emcha, Tayaima

&

Eche Memcha

Preface

The book explores the political aspirations of the tri-ethnic community of Manipur, the Meiteis, the Nagas and the Kuki-Chin, in order to analyse the political implication at the backdrop of identity, identity crisis and politics of identity. Also, efforts have been made to understand the dynamic changes in the politicisation process by the external forces like religion from outside, British colonialism and existing political system which led to assertion of interests and relations among the various ethnic groups as spiral in character and how it becomes to claim periphery within periphery. After merge to Indian union in 1949, various insurgent groups have been comings up to retain the lost sovereignty. This directly leads to witnessing the ongoing political violence for the last six decades. It is said that Manipur is paradise for the anthropologists and politically it is hotbed. Furthermore, there is a big question 'where is the hidden paradise on earth where the god and goddess are dancing?'

Moreover, if we look back to her glorious past, people have lived together in an atmosphere of love, care and mutual sharing of responsibilities. And they look forward to live happily forever. However, this glorious past seems to be threatened to extinction by the animosities among the hill and the plain people of the present days. Much of that the existing conditions of hill and that of plain peoples spell out continuous conflicts, misunderstandings and miseries, not only among the people of the respective tribes and groups but also for the governments of the nation. In these situations of conflict, it is possible to initiate the actions that would restore the glorious past and revive the traditions of peaceful co-existence and accommodation of vested interest. The question could be answered only by studying with a detailed probing in this area and that is the thrust of this book.

For a clear understanding of emerging conflict situation of Manipur, the genesis of it is traced and it is the concomitant identity crisis with its political implications. Identity crisis means an acute anxiety state experienced by a person or group who finds it difficult to establish a clearly defined personal or group identity. Whenever there occurs a phase or period seeking new set of definition amidst unclear role choices of an individual or group, there occurs the psycho-social phenomenon of identity crisis. Such phenomenons have occurred in the socio-political situation of Manipur.

The objective of taking up this study is to produce a comprehensive and critical analysis of claiming periphery within periphery and its political activities behind it. Different socialisation process with different political culture in hill and valley and the crux of democratic institution without democratic politics are intended to be explored. The book also analyses 'unity through criticism' towards understanding accumulated discontentment of both hill and valley, because it creates ethnic nationalism with ethnic armies.

For the sake of convenience, the book has been divided into chapters on the basis of different elements of its originations. Chapter I deals with conceptual study of identity, identity crisis and politics of identity. Chapter II deals with an intention to explore the common origin of the people who were inhabited in Manipur since time immemorial and how plurality leads to the crisis of identity. Chapter III tries to throw light about the emergence of tribal identity with their expansion movement, the changing dynamics and its repercussion in a very systematic way. Chapter IV deals with demanding of homeland like Southern Nagaland and struggle of Kukis for Kuki homeland. Chapter V is dedicated to the study of the Self-determination, external as well as internal. In this chapter assertion and reaction of interest, emergence of communal politics and accommodation of interest are focused in detail for arriving at an amicable solution. The VI and final chapter which forms a conclusion of the book gives a summary of the preceding chapters. In addition, it tries to fulfills the stated aims of the book as well as substantiate the argument and propositions that the political aspirations of the people in the state have been to fight against the structural injustice which is actually a manifestation and overt expression of having democratic institutions without democratic politics. It also gives recommendations and suggestions to overcome the whole issue.

It is based mainly on Government and official publications, documents like pamphlets, press notes, leaflets and other publications. Besides, interview with a quite number of activists, academicians, scholars who by virtue of their experience of dealing with the dynamics of inter-group relations and the issue related with the study cutting across community lines proved to be of great help, thereby forming and supplementing a part of experienced survey.

I express my sincere gratitude, humble regards and thanks to Dr. Dhanabir Laishram for his thought provoking ideas and revealing insights to complete this work. I also extend my regards to Mr. D. Kumar of Anshah Publishing House for bringing out the book in time.

Last but not the least, I extend my profound gratitude to my family members especially Tachou for his innumerable support, co-operation, cheerful affection and words of encouragement in my efforts. Furthermore, I can't but recall the memory of my beloved Ech'emcha, Tayaima and Eche – Memcha who were always with me for the cause of my study during their lifetime. Further any omission, commission arises are completely mine.

Ch. Rupachandra Singh

Contents

Abbreviation

ATSUM	:	All Tribal Students Union Manipur
ANSAM	:	All Naga Students Association Manipur
COFPAI	:	Committee for Peace and Integrity
CHIKIM	:	Chin Kuki Mizo
FGN	:	Federal Government of Nagaland
IDEA	:	International Institute for Demo-cracy and Electoral Assistance
KNO	:	Kuki National Organisation
KNA	:	Kuki Nationa Assembly
KNA	:	Kuki National Army
KNF	:	Kuki National Front
LS	:	Lok Sabha
MNF	:	Mizo National Front
MMU	:	Mao Maram Union
MNC	:	Manipur Naga Council
MNF	:	Mizo National Front

MPC	:	Mizo Peoples Convention
MP	:	Member of Parliament
MPRA	:	Manipur Panchayati Raj Act
MSCA	:	Manipur State Constitution Act
MZU	:	Manipur Zeliangrong Union
MPC	:	Mizo-People's Convention
NE	:	North East
NEPI	:	North East Peoples Initiative
NFA	:	Naga Federal Army
NHDTC	:	Naga Hills District Tribal Council
NPOC	:	Naga Peace Organising Committee
NPC	:	Naga People's Convention
NPC	:	Nagaland Peace Council
NNC	:	Naga National Council
NRC	:	National Research Centre
NSCN	:	National Socialist Council of Nagaland
NSCN-IM	:	National Socialist Council of Nagaland – Isaac- Muivah
NSCN-K	:	National Socialist Council of Nagaland –Khaplang
NNL	:	Naga National League
NPOC	:	Naga Peace Organising Committee
SNUNS	:	Southern Naga Union of Nagaland States
SoO	:	Suspension of Operation
UNC	:	United Naga Council

I
Introduction

The term 'Identity' and its associated terms like 'Identity Crisis,' 'Politics of Identity' now enjoy immense popularity in many parts of the world. Identity is a key word not only in the theoretical and political discourse but also in everyday parlance. It is also necessary to think why such perception and its disorders are spreading throughout the third and fourth world people.[1] They are getting both depression and menace in this crisis. Uncountable people of the world particularly in fourth world are getting forced assimilation, human rights violation, loss of their ancestral land, transfer of population etc. Besides claiming periphery within periphery itself, they have become refugees in their own native land after conceiving the idea of protecting their identities. So they are in the crisis of conflict situation which lead to the creation of internal contradiction.

Like occurring across the world in Rwanda, Bosnia, Kosovo and elsewhere, the people of north-east India in general and Manipur in particular are in deep waves of this identity issues. It becomes more and more complex to India's north-east region where more than 200 ethnic minorities are felling insecurity to the present context. So they are in the process of conflict management, conflict transformation and conflict resolution. Basically, these are the consequence of identity crisis. We have to see its conceptual study and how far it is related with political discourse. The International Institute for Democracy and Electoral Assistance (IDEA) in one of its report cited that some 80 per cent of major conflicts in the 1990s had a clear identity component. In this 'clear identity component', secession is only the means for that. So their alternative frame is independent.[2] Thus, for a clear comprehensive understanding of the issues with reference to Manipur we need to see the concept of identity, identity crisis and how it leads to the politics of identity.

Identity and Identity Crisis

The definition of a concept in any field of social sciences is generally problematic in regarding with its terminology, usages etc. And the term such as 'Identity' loaded with meanings, values and prejudices are even more difficult to define. This word was originated from the Latin word 'idem' which literally meant 'sameness' arouses from the notion of something always being itself (rather than something else).[3] It is used in most of the discipline of social sciences to describe a person's conception and expression of his/her individuality or group affiliations (such as national identity and cultural identity). The term is used more specifically in psychology and sociology. It also gives a great deal of attention in social psychology and social anthropology.

Erickson defines it as 'a subjective sense as well as an observable quality, paired with some belief in the sameness and continuity of some shared world image'.[4] He perceives it as a multifaceted notion form by the interrelations of the individuals with their social surroundings and refers to 'a persistent sameness within oneself (self-sameness) and sharing of some kind of essential character with other'.[5] It is the state or fact remaining the same one or ones under the varying conditions and circumstances that the feeling of sameness and continuity of an individual or group that his or their past purposes and values, experiences and belief in a common future belong to him or to them. It is also the experience of an individual or group, a recognisable continuous and persistent entity and it is what one thinks about himself as the 'real me.'

Further, the word 'identity' means the quality or condition of being the same in substance, composition, nature, properties or in particular qualities under consideration, absolute or essential sameness or oneness.[6] In some discipline like philosophy, it means sameness as distinguished from the change or difference. It has been a term of interest to philosophers chiefly in connection with the problem of universal and the law of identity in logic.[7] Again, identity is not a core sociological concept in spite of its frequent occurrence in the everyday vocabulary of sociologists. Even in the substantive areas, such as the study of ethnicity, where we can observe the use of the term with great frequency, identity has not received sustained analytical attention, in the sense of locating it in conceptual contents and shaping it to much more than connotative significance.[8]

Moreover as a norm, the social group speaking a language and possessing common cultural tradition tend to develop a close association more quickly. The individual level contacts at the initial stage lead to a large scale contacts even through the exchange of spouses and involvements in various socio-economic activities. In most cases, this process ultimately leads to the acceptance of common Identity. Thus, Identity of a society appears to be a summation of what individuals have given to the society and society sustains its identity through a continuous projection of infinite space and time. It can also broadly characterise as the process by which an individual is bound to his or her social self and this sense is a very natural human tendency.

The formation or construction of Identities is mainly based on various traits and experiences of the individual or the group concerned. It would be culture, religion, race, region, language, ethnicity etc. Here mention may be made of cultural identity as it is the feeling of an individual or group where he or she is influenced by him or her belonging to a group or culture. It is a social process in which individuals participate, in the idea of changing historical conditions. As a 'historical reservoir,' culture is an important factor in shaping identity.[9] Though there arises many questions on culture in regarding the formation of identity. Again the formation of an ethnic identity is the recognition with a certain ethnicity, usually on the basis of an assumed common genealogy or ancestry. Recognition by others as a distinct ethnic group is often a contributing factor to developing these bonds of identification. These groups are also often united by common cultural, behavioural, linguistics' or religious traits.

The process of this identity formation comes to a decisive crisis in the youth—a crisis get alleviated or aggravated by different societies in different ways.[10] It is not the function of a single process, various endogenous and exogenous forces influence in building the affinities and attachments that make identity formation a complex process. The development in this process has fused with each other in a sense of sameness and continuity. Then the persistent infantile identification are brought in line with urgent new serve definitions and irreversible role of choices, these develop the identity crisis. To Erickson, the development of self-identity meets a catalyst—an identity crisis around adolescences or early adulthood.[11]

The concept of 'crisis' is a lay term in searching for a scholarly meaning. Literally Greek meaning of turning point or time of decision is used by anthropologists, historians, sociologist, political scientist, psychologists etc. Therefore, if a crisis in any process is just a turning point, then identity crisis is turning point in the process of one's or group's existence and also that distinguishes the outcome of an event favorably or unfavorably, between life and death, violence or non-violence and resolution or protracted conflict. Erickson regards crisis as inevitable in the development of identity of the individuals.[12] He observes that crisis means 'a crucial time or an inescapable turning point for better or worse'. 'Better' here means a confluence of constructive energy of the individuals or society and 'Worse' means prolonged identity confusions in young individuals or in society.[13] Thus, it is an acute anxiety state experience by a person or group who finds it difficult to establish a clearly defined personal or group identity.

For instance there occurs a phase or period seeking new set of definitions amidst unclear role choices of an individual or group; there occurs the psycho-social phenomenon of identity crisis. Theoretically it becomes a time of intensive analysis and exploration of different ways of looking at oneself or themselves. According to Erickson, this term was first used for a specific clinical purpose in the Mt. Zion rehabilitation clinic during the Second World War, a natural emergency which permitted psychiatric workers of different persuasions and denominations to work together harmoniously.[14] It becomes a term with popular and scientific usages which alternately circumscribe something to large and so seemingly self-evident that to demand definition would almost seem pity, while at other times they designate something made so narrow for purpose of measurement that the overall meaning is large and it could just as well be called something else.[15] Therefore it is recurring phenomenon in the socio-political development of a group or a community.

In every new generation, there is always a demand and confirm positive identity to regenerate itself and preserve. With the emergence of pluralism, post modernity and breakdown of traditional social structure, in contrast to the earlier momentary crisis depicted by Erickson, the state of crisis is ongoing and endemic throughout the individual life or society.[16] It is also opened up to focus on distinctive forms of social identity based on the ethnicity, gender, youth and nationality.

Moreover controversial efforts, which were made by both—Fakuyama on 'The End of History' and Samuel P Huntington on 'The Clash of Civillisation,' focused on the central theme that culture and cultural identities which at the broadest level are civilisational identities where it is shaping the pattern of cohesion, disintegration, and conflict. In Huntington's debate, one could see basic assumption of clash in concepts such as 'pluralistic,' 'modernisation' and 'consequences.' The same theme could be applied in the context of Manipur also.

For instance, the concept of Manipuri nationalism could not be receptacle to the hill and ethnic pluralism and its commonness would not be beyond the argument in the mindset of all major ethnic groups of Manipur. It has common national identity since the formation of this nation centuries ago. Although it is argued that national identity is not an inborn trait. It is a direct result of the presence of the various manifestation for the construction or formation of identity like common ancestry, national symbols, language, the nation's roots of history, national consciousness, blood ties, culture etc. So national identity is the person's or group's identity and is sense of belonging to one state or to one nation, a feeling one shares with a group of people, regardless of one's citizenship status. The sense of this belongingness to the nation is essential as an external threat becomes clearer.[17]

In other words, civilisation and modernism give negative tacit values to them. They are heeding in revenging attitude by modifying the past history without facts. It also leads them to make cultural forces and ferment as they think about ethnic nationalism and racial boundary. So the present discourse is based on political implications of it. We have social, ethnic or cultural identity of communities and national identity. Various cultural studies and social theory investigate the question of cultural and ethnic identities. Cultural identity basically observes upon the place, gender, race, history, nationality, sexual orientation, religious beliefs and ethnicity whereas national identity is an ethical and philosophical concept where all humans are divided into groups called nations. Members of a nation share a common identity and usually a common origin in the sense of ancestry, parentage or descent.

Likewise, a social identity of an ethnic group includes their common past or history, cultural heritage, linguistic affinity, their shared experiences, struggle and suffering with a strong sense of belonging to each other and identification with ideology and a belief in the common future. It is a part of an individual's or group's perceptions that arises from 'the individual's knowledge that he belongs to certain groups together with some emotional and value significance to him of this membership'.[18] In this social identity there is no crisis among the various ethnic groups of Manipur, because they are from the same ancestors having close ties of blood relationship. But the cleavages which are being visualized are an outcome of the external forces and crisis of nationalism.

Politics of Identity

Identity politics are political arguments that focus upon the self-interest and perspectives of self-identified interest groups and ways in which people's politics may be shaped by aspects of their identity through race, class, religion, ethnicity or traditional dominance. Though, not all members of any given group are necessarily involved in identity politics. It is mostly based on the politics of group marginalisation fracturing the civil polity, and therefore work against creating real opportunities for ending marginalisation. Religious identity is also one of the basic foundations of identity politics. In the name of nationalism various political parties, civil society organisations have launched political mobilisation along the religious line to play identity politics.

But the consequences of identity politics in Manipur now-a-days become to weaken and disrupt the common movement which is necessary to build up against the marginalisation and social deprivation. In this era of post modernism, it had weakened the common movement by creating the differences between the people or groups but did not touch the establishment. Thus, post modernism goes with identity including with its multifaceted predicaments.

However, ethnic identity politics is different from others. The remarkable examples were seen in India's north east. There were mass killings between different ethnic groups although they have propagated same religion and speaking same language. Each of the different ethnic groups had their ethnic consciousness based on their own interest. It would be seen from the early part of 80s as there were ups and down in the common platform or issues where different ethnic group began to play as it led to the worst situation ever in the history of political identity in the region. The Assamese, Khasis, Manipuris, Mizos or Nagas may have form majority in their own respective state but those minority groups residing within the geographical boundary of the state had geared up to feel insecurity. Even within the Nagas of Nagaland such feelings were comes up. Therefore it leads to the politics of identity.

In Manipur these led to witness the ethnic clashes between the two major ethnic groups from the early part of 90s. This ethnic identity and narrow nationalism based on their consciousness had brought the situation of the state in conundrum. The highway politics as a tool for achieving their demand on some vested interests had kept other communities in hostages. In the preceding years it is seen that the so called only two lifelines had blocked on several occasions. Here it is said that out of 365 days, more than 120 days in a calendar year had blocked.

The demand of district re-organisation added further turmoil in the identity politics. The demanding of district of the Sadar hills sub-division and Jiribam sub-division had further added oil in the flames. Other communities had felt uncertain on the ground of the inclusion of their territory on the demand and these would not be the ending points. Further it is assumed that there would come up the demands of Tipaimukh, Phungyar, Tongjei Maril, Tengnoupal etc. And if Sadar hills got its demand fulfilled then there would be demand for Liangmei within the Sadar hills.

Therefore, people have been demanding to reorganise the territorial district on the basis to accommodate the aspiration of different communities and not on the basis of electoral gains that government has so far taken up. Prolonged blocked of the lifeline by those communities residing nearby of it would further irritate other communities and this is the politics of identity played on the ethnic lines. Sometimes identity politics become a basis of separatism in the region, therefore government tries to pacify those minority ethnic groups by granting autonomy to some extent. Some of those get a separate entity as a state but in this little paradise with a of population of 27 lakhs or little more, would it be a long term solution to create states within this state is the dilemma. It is from the early part of 80s where there emerge the issues of identity politics in the state. It brings animosity between different communities who have been residing in this place since time immemorial. The consecutive governments did not act in the right time and this further consolidated the old wounds. Hence, it is better to trace back their ancestral relationship and compelled to see how far the crisis of nationalism gives acute anxiety to the people and keep them in the turning point for better or worse.

Notes and References

1. Four types of people could be classified in the world today. They are first world people (capitalist countries of Europe and America) 2nd world people, communist countries of the world, 3rd world people means Asia and African people who are under developed and got independence during the last few decades, 4th world people, on the other hand denote the people who could not represent in the UN. They are also known as indigenous people.
2. David Bloomfield and Ben Reilly (eds.); *'Institute for Democracy and Electoral Assistance (IDEA), Democracy and Deep rooted Conflict: Options for Negotiators,'* Stockholm: International IDEA, 1998, p. 4.
3. Ayto, John; *'Bloomsbury Dictionary of Word Origin,'* 86, UB Delhi. Goyal Jawahar Nagar Saab, 1st Indian edition, 75 editions, 1990, pp. 292-93.
4. Erikson, E.H.; 'Reflections on the dissent of contemporary youth,' *International Journal of Psychoanalysis, 51,* 1970; pp. 11-22.
5. Erickson, E.H.; *Identity and the Life Cycle: Selected Papers,* New York; International University press.1959.
6. JA Simpson and E.S.C. Weiner (eds.); *'The Oxford English Dictionary,'* Oxford: Clarendon Press, 1989, second edition, vol. V11, p. 620.
7. Danbury; *'The Encyclopedia Americana,'* International edition, Grolier Incorporated, 1999, p. 743.
8. Roland Robertson and Burkart Holzner; 'Identity and Authority: A Problem Analysis of process of identification'

in Roland Robertson Burkart Holzner (Eds.), *Identity and Authority*, Oxford: Basil Blackwell, 1980, p. 2.

9. Pratt, Nicola; 'Identity, Culture and Democratization: The Case of Egypt,' *New Political Science*, 27 (1): 2005; pp. 69-86.
10. 'Identity and Sexuality: A study of their interrelationship in men.' *Journal of the American psychoanalytic Association*: 9, 1954, pp. 176-260.
11. *Op.cit.*, '*Identity and Life Cycle: Selected Papers.*'
12. Sills, David L.; '*International Encyclopedia of Social Sciences*,' vol. 3 and vol. 4, New York, McMillan Company and Free Press, 1972, p. 513.
13. Erickson, E.H.; '*Young Man Luther*,' New York, Norton, 1958.
14. Erickson, E.H.; '*Identity: Youth and Crisis*,' 3 Queen Square, London, Faber and Faber: 1971, pp. 16-17.
15. *Ibid.* p. 15.
16. Lash, Scott and Jonathan Friedman (eds.), '*Modernity and Identity*,' Oxford and Cambridge. Massachusetts, Blackwell, 1992, p. 12.
17. See Anthony D. Smith; *National identity (Ethno nationalism in Comparative Perspective)* University of Nevada Press, 1993.
18. Tajfel, edited by Henri (2010); '*Social identity and intergroup relations*' (1. Paperback printing ed.). Cambridge: Cambridge University Press, p. 2.

II
Common Origin

We have lot of literature about the genealogy of the origin of the Manipuri people regarding its common ancestry. Manipur comprises a plural society, consisting of three major ethnic groups namely the Meitei[1], the Naga[2] and the Kuki-Chin[3] with various migrant communities and Manipuri's Muslims known as Meitei Pangals. Both the Meitei and Meitei Pangal are in the valley and majority of the Nagas and the Kuki-Chin's people were in the hill. These 'Naga' and 'Kuki-Chin' are the generic terms given by the administrators of the British India government and those anthropologists of by gone days for their convenience. These tribes have got a number of tribes, sub-tribes, clans, sub-clans, lineages and sub-lineages.

Most of the people basically outsiders harbor the notion that Meiteis have only one entity. So they differently perceive Meiteis and tribals. Although for the valley people, the term Meitei is applicable to anyone belonging to the seven clans that are composed of 'Mangang' also known as 'Ningthouja,' 'Luwang,' 'Khuman,' 'Angom,' 'Moirang,' 'Khaba-Nganba' and 'Sarang Leisangthem.' Out of these seven clans except Mangang, most of them were scattering as highlanders in the prehistory period. Therefore the so called Nagas, Kuki-Chin's and other sub tribes were same as Meitei in origin. Various theories had been come up in regarding the common originality of these major ethnic groups. Roland Shimmi observes that the seven original Meiteis clans or tribes and the Nagas are racially one.[4] These seven clans had their own respective territories, population and kings, who ruled over their clan members. They were commonly known as seven independent communities. These clans fought with each other for acquiring more land, resources, wealth and men. Conquest and annexation amongst themselves continued for a very long period. First of all Khaba-Nganba and Sarang-Leisangthem were merged to the Mangang/Ningthouja (population of both clans were very few because most of them inhabited in the hill areas) and then Luwang and Angom followed suit. The Khuman reigned up to 12th century and was subdued by the Meitei (Mangang/Ningthouja came to be known as Meitei), and Moirang was completely conquered and subdued in the 18th century.[5]

After 18th century all the seven clans were united as one group commonly known as Meitei. Before the beginning of 19th century, all the highlanders of Manipur were ruled by their chief. In reality these tribal people were some of the clans of Meitei. Majority of them were 'Khaba-Nganba' and 'Sarang Leisangthem'. They were Kabui, Tangkhul, Maring, Khongsai and Anal.[6] Again Roland Shimmi observes the Meitei clan Khaba Nganba in every probability is the Khapainao or Kapainao clan of the Thangkhul.[7] They settled to the hill for many reasons. The Meitei king completely subdued almost all of them and Manipur was brought under the sovereignty of one king. Thus all are come to one umbrella known as Manipuri's (most of the Meitei people want to call it as Meitei or Meetei. But it is better to call Manipuri in order to have integral name because Manipuri mean to those people who were inhabited in Manipur). But the people of Manipur are confronting the problem of ethnic pluralism canvass to the highlanders. Highlanders intentionally refuted to being Manipuris. They were very much in anguish that the king did not launch such ethnic pluralism canvass to the highlanders in the right time.

Some people argued that it was a big tragedy of hill and valley people because if this canvasses should be done successfully; there will be no intervention of Hindu Vaishnavism or other exogenous religion. The subsequent result is the cleavage between hill and valley obviously. As a consequent fall out, the highlanders are compelled to identify themselves as belonging to either Naga or Kuki. This does not and need not mean the integration of hill and valley resulting in the emergence of a new single and social amalgam in place of the existing two. As long as the dichotomy of hill and valley exists, there will continue to be two societies with individual characteristics. But there should be no hurdles and obstacles to prevent the generation of forces that would make for a symbiotic relationship between the two for enabling them to mix better.

Like Meitei unification of seven clans, highlanders are also very busy to keep the same carbon copy of Meitei. They want to unite all the different tribes in one group as Nagas and Kuki-Chin, but it is very far from the unification of their brethrens like the Meiteis. They are compelled to do, because they have so many groups such as Anal, Aimol, Chiru, Chothe, Gangte, Hmar, Kabui, Kacha Naga, Koirao, Koireng, Kom, Lamkang, Mizo, Lushai, Maram, Maring, Mao, Monsang, Moyon, Paite, Ralte, Sema, Simte, Salhte, Tangkhul, Thadou, Vaiphei, Zou etc. Besides these there were also unspecified groups.

Though the Naga and Kuki-Chin have their separate cultures, customs, traditions, languages, manners, beliefs, rites and rituals, method and cultivation, forms of government, they share the same origin with Meitei and also possess common ancestors with same historical roots.

Historical Roots

Most of the outsiders leave Manipur after conceiving the idea that plainsmen and highlanders of Manipur remain different from each other, because they eat differently, dress differently and even tend to think differently. It is also mainly influenced by the geographical factor that one-tenth of the total area is valley and the remaining is made up of hills. These areas are having unsound communication and not developed in all fields in comparison with valley. It creates the idea of differences and it has been sharpened by the feelings that they are two social organisms diametrically opposite to each other. They seem always do and have been doing so. The majority Meitei have to know the composition of Manipuris and tribals also have to trace back their ancestry. Both the inhabitants had contributed their sweat and blood to the growth of Manipuri civilisation. In short, Manipur is the home of tribals as it is of the Meiteis.

The budding scholars of Manipur concerned with the welfare and overcoming the ills plague in present scenario had always been putting labour to find out the different social streams of Meitei and 'Chingmee' (Hill dwellers) from the early history of Manipur who can pick up different elements of Meitei-Tribal social norms in the past.[8] Therefore they have to identify 'who are they' with the help of our history. The terms 'Naga' and 'Kuki' are non-existent in the olden days of Manipur history. All are from Meitei clans except a few groups who came to Manipur in the later part of Manipur history.[9]

The history of Manipur was the story of relationship between hill and valley. It is too long, so even today, people have illusion that they are not from common ancestry. So the highlanders always speak for themselves and not for others as it indicates that they did not try to trace back the relationship. It is natural in one sense because they have not written any documents and history. They were migrated to the hill and their forefathers inhabited in the valley, practically all should confine in the valley due to several reasons. Moreover valley people were known as 'Tamme' and hill folk were known as 'Chingmee' and they were from the same ancestry[10] that is why both valley and hill people are same. T.C. Hudson observes, 'Two hundred years ago, in the internal organization, in religion, in habits and manners, the Meiteis were as the hill people as now are.'[11] In short, they were having close ties of blood relationship. They are brothers and sisters of a family and it is proved beyond doubt by the historical background of this little paradise.

Different legends had assumed the highlanders and the valley people are common ancestry. According to one such story still being retold in Manipur, the whole valley came under deluge during the pre-historic period.[12] The people living in the valley fled to the hills and lived there as long as the floods lasted. When the time came to return to the plains, some of them stayed on the hill and others came back to their original habitat. The people of the valley thus got divided into the hill folk and the plains' folk. They were practising inter-marriage between them. The first king of Manipur Nongda Lairen Pakhangba married a highlander Laishna, it is not a hill folk name but likely the prince gave her a name of his choice. Another king also married a tribal girl known as Linthoi Ngambi and it happened during the beginning of the 15th century.[13] King Paikhomba also took Ingallei, daughter of Maram Khullakpa as his wife. It means most of the rulers of Manipur were the direct blood relations of the tribal. And still this social practice of inter-marriage is going on among the hill and valley people. There was no caste system during the pre-Hindu period of Manipur. Even today caste system is not in practice in Manipur, and instead of this there is class system.

The early Meetei population may be broadly classified into three categories, the noble, the commoners and the slave.[14] Nobility was not hereditary for all sections of the population and one could become a noble if he/she received recognition and favour of the king and also tribal chiefs got it. During the time of Pamheiba (1709-1740), the ministers and the Sardars of Manipur used to receive tribal chiefs quite frequently and dealt with them as good friends. The slaves on the other hand did not comprise as separate community or group, though the tribals claim they were used by the king as slave of him. They were mainly discharging their duties for royal family members and nobles. Both Meiteis and tribal were working under this category. But slavery institution in Manipur was different from that of other parts of the world. They lived in the same house as their master, ate with him and were altogether like members of the family. The valley and the hills also had the same food habits. Before Vaishnavite came, the meat was the best part of the valley's menu.

They had inter-dinning from very early period of history. King Charairongba invited the different tribal chiefs to the grand feasts. His son Pamheiba made the great days of hill valley entente, almost a close thing to harmony. He liked other rulers ascended the throne in tribal costume. He did not arrange the royal feasts without inviting the chiefs of the hills. In short the

Meiteis had similar habits, manners, customs and beliefs with Naga people before contact with other advanced groups and adoption of Hinduism.[16]

Again Manipur have a recorded history of coronation only from 33 A.D. during the reign of Nongda Leiren Pakhangba. Before him, it was ruled by the leader of Khaba clan (one of the clan of the Meitei). It can be traced with the help of some chronicles, ancient text of Manipur such as Panthoibi Khongul, Chakpa Khunda Khunthok and Pakhangba Laihui etc. His name was Khaba Sokchrongba and Panthoibi was his daughter-in-law.[17] This clan was very powerful before 33 A.D. But another king, successor of Khaba whose name was Nongchenba fought with Pakhangba of Ningthouja clan. Pakhangba was defeated and took refuge at Moirang. He got two children namely Mungyang Chaoba and Tangkrumlumyiba. Then Pakhangba attacked the king Nongchenba and killed in the battlefield. Most of the Khaba people fled away to take shelter in different parts of Manipur. Some Khaba converted as Kabui Nungna, some were as Tangkhul and Mahou Lontai, and some of them were mixing with Angom clan. Lastly, the king Khaba Nonganba surrendered to the king Nongda Lairen Pakhangba.[18]

Moreover, there was a story of the leader of Sarang Leisangthem who also landed on the hill and lived as highlanders. He belonged to the Kabui clan. The same case also happened to the Khuman clan. Most of the Khuman people also inhabited in the hill as Maring. The names of the Khuman leaders were, the last sons of Sanaba Meemaba, Thingol Likmaba, Khamlangba and his son Khayingba. According to Manipur's ancient text 'Tutenglon,' most of the Moirang people were settled on the Koubru hills and the people of Selloi Langmai on the Nongmaiching hills.[19] They were practicing inter-marriage among them. During the deluge of Manipur, Meitei ningthou Khuyoi Tompok and his wife Nongmainu Ahongbi had three children, Yoymongba, Taothingmang and Lairok Lembi. Lairok Lembi was married to the king Anganga of Koubru hill and settled to the Koubru hills with his brothers. Thus people of different clans scattered from valley to the hills of Manipur. So they are the members of a same family having a pure blood relationship.

In case of Kuki according to Daltion, it consists of old and new Kukis. The old and new Kukis are obviously of the same race and point of divergence arises merely from their having settled or migrated at different periods and stages of history. The Kukis are now found as neighbours of Nagas in Assam and scattered in northern Cachar, Manipur and across the border in Myanmar and Bangladesh. They are often described as a nation of hunters and warriors. They rule as a nation by their principal hereditary chiefs.

According to Grierson, the term new Kuki may be taken as synonymous with Thadou clan. The clan is very large and Thadou entered Manipur hills at about the middle of 18th century. It give confusion to the Meitei because only the British who divided the people living in the hill areas into Nagas and Kukis. Further they divided Kukis as old Kuki and new Kuki, like as Naga and Kacha Nagas.

But the question is what about of Taothingmang, son of Meitei king Khuyoi Tompok, who might be ruler between 158-264 AD. Taothingmang with his brother Yoymongba took shelter to the Koubru hills as it was ruled by their brother-in-law, Anganga (who was also coming from Moirang) during the time of deluge.[20] It might had happened between the years of 264 to 364 AD. They were settling on this hill as Khongsai (valley people prefer to call Kuki as Khongsai). Lizangnee Gangte claimed that Naothingkhong and Khongtekcha were also Thadou kings.[21] Kukis also have their legend that they were settling in the valley. But they could no longer continue to live in what they called the upper valley (Phaichungung) due to devastating flood; they call it 'Tutobin'. As a result, most of the Khongsai (Thadou) migrated to the hills.

W. Mc Culloch observes that the major tribes and clans of the Meitei have been the descendants of the Naga and Kuki tribes.[22] It means he studied the relationship between hill and valley people in the later period when they stayed here. If he analyses links with all these past incidents, he should have said or remarked that the major tribes of Naga and Kuki are the descendants of the Meiteis. In other words, it needs to ponder again and deep retrospection towards understanding such relationship instead of giving flying bird's views. In order to strengthen and commemorate this relationship, the people of Manipur have been performing the function of 'Mera Houchongba' since time immemorial. In this festival most of the highlanders with their chiefs are coming to the palace in every October (Mera) and performing many traditional activities, cultural items and grand feast.

Pluralism and Identity Crisis

It is a natural phenomenon that various ethnic groups had to try to make relevant with the changing situations and encounters. Different ethnic groups had asserted their ethnicity in social, economic and political development. Thus ethnicity becomes a very decisive force in the identity formation of the Nagas and Kuki-Chin groups. But among the Meiteis, it had ceased to be an effective force after the attainment of nationhood and nation state.[23] This ethnic pluralism become the root cause of the absence of common identity of the people of Manipur and it leads to the identity crisis more complex.[24]

The genesis of the identity crisis can be traced to the Sanskritisation of Manipur, British colonialism, Christian evangelism among the hill tribes, Manipur's merger into Indian union and emergence of tribal solidarity movements. It is undisputed fact that for the hill people as a whole, the political headquarters remained in the valley. Due to having foreign aggression and occasional rebellion, highlanders accepted the valley king as the lord of the valley and hill as well. The king of the valley was the only person to maintain peace and security to both the hill and valley people. His writ ran not only in the hills now forming parts of Manipur but even beyond it towards the present artificial boundary. Mention could be made of present day Nagaland, according to Col. Johnstone, all the villages in the present Nagaland had Manipuri's names in addition to their own. Nagaland is known to Manipuri's as 'Thibongmei.' King Gambhir Singh (1825-34) reduced several villages in the Naga Hills including Kohima where he stood on a stone and had his footprint sculptured on it, in token of conquest.[25] The Nagas greatly respected this stone and cleaned it from time to time.[26] But, it was blasted by bomb and is now kept in the archives into its pieces. It was blasted by the Naga ultras to make confusion of Manipur boundary expanded by the king. Col. Johnstone says that the people of Manipur valley (Meitei) could go to any village in the former Naga Hills and be sure of warm hospitality at a time while the British, venturing into these areas unprotected, ran the risk of being murdered.

A group of Nagas went to Imphal in a delegation and requested the king to take them into the Hindu fold. But the Hindu Brahma Sabha of the palace gave the negative response on the ground that a 'Hindu is born, never made.'[27] The king of Manipur refused to do so, in the sense that he could not influence the Brahma Sabha. The conversion of Vaishnavism Hindu of Meitei took place during the reign of Pamheiba though the great objection was made by the peoples and 'Maichous' (they constitutes the class of nobility who by virtue of their knowledge act as advisor of the sovereign in the temporal as well as religious affairs) of valley.

This was the crucial period of hill-valley relationship. Hodson observes, 'the successive waves of foreign invasion, Shan, Burmese, English, Hindu had left each permanent marks on the civilization of the people so that they have finally passed away from the stage of primitive culture into one of comparative civilization, but their ultimate homogeneity with the Nagas and Kukis of the hills is undoubted and in my opinion needs no further insistence.'[28] The social intimacy of hill-valley people parted ways by the rigid norms of Vaishnavite Hinduism. Even today also Meiteis are not Vaisnavites completely. Some section of the people of the valley went a bit far from king jurisdiction and remained as original valley people. They were known as 'Lois' and they are not having any different characteristic with today's non-Christian tribal. In short they were having the same religion, set of habits, customs and manners, the vestige of which is still to be found in non-Christian Naga villages of today.[29]

Due to having rigid principles of Vaishnavism, it created a rift and the ever widening cleavages among the hill and valley. Things gradually began to fall in place and the crust of conservatism started breaking. When Sanskritisation of the Meitei society and state in the 18th century begun, the conversion into Hinduism was set rolling in the royalty and the common people, deliberate attempts were made to give a new identity to the people and kingdom of the Meiteis. The kingdom was renamed 'Manipur' according to 'Sanamahi Laikan' in 1724 AD, and a new genealogy of the royal family was prepared tracing its origin to the Aryan group of people who were classified as the Kshetriya caste. The religious syncretism between traditional Meitei religion with new Hinduism was brought out. This Sanskritisation process created more confusion due to the identification of religion with racial or ethnic origin.

Notes and References

1. Meitei composed of seven clans-Mangang, Luwang, Khuman, Angom, Moirang, Khaba-Nganba, and Sarang-Leisangthem. Mangang is also known as Ningthouja.
2. Naga-today in the Nagaisation process the following ethnic groups becomes Naga. They are Aimol, Anal, Angami, Aao, Chakesang, Chang, Chiru, Chothe, Kharam, Khiamnuingam, Koireng, Konyak, Laimung, Lamkang, Lotha, Mao, Maram, Maring, Makhori, Monsang, Moyon, Noete, Pangmei, Phom, Pochury, Poumei, Rengma, Sangtam, Sema, Tangkhul, Tangsa, Tarao, Thangal, Wancho, Yimchunger and Zeliangrong.
3. Kuki-Chin; it is also a nomenclature given by the British; it has three groups Old Kuki, New-Kuki and Kuki-Chin. In the old-Kuki, Aimol, Anal, Chiru, Chothe, Gangte, Kairou, Koireng, Kom, Lamgang, Paite, Purum, Simte, Vaiphei, Zou and Hmar are included; in the new-Kuki, Thadou (Doungel, Misao, Lupheng, Lupho, Ngeilu, Lamhao, Thangeo and Taothag) are included, Kuki-Chin group comprised of Thadou, Paite, Gangte, Simte, Vaiphei, Sahte, Zou, Hmar and Mizo.
4. Shimmi, Y. L. Roland; '*Comparative History of Nagas; from Ancient Period till 1826,*' New Delhi, Inter India Publications, 1988. p. 118

5. Ibungohal, L.; '*Introduction to Manipur,*' Imphal.1987, p. 10.
6. Khelchandra; '*Ching Amasung Tamgi Mari,*' unpublished article.
7. *Op.cit.*, '*Comparative History of Nagas; from Ancient Period till 1826,*' p. 86.
8. Dhanabir Laishram, '*Chaokhatpa Khunnai Amasung Meeyam,*' Imphal, 2000, p. 6.
9. Personal interviewed with N. Khelchandra dt. 21, May, 2004, he stated that all the hill folk are from the Meitei clans.
10. According to Kriti Tensuba, all of us were coming from the Yunnan province of China, settling at the river bank of the Huwangho River.
11. Hodson, T.C.; '*The Meithei's,*' New Delhi, Low Price Publications, 1999, p. 11.
12. The valley areas of Manipur were under water at one time is a fact on which Geologists almost agreed.
13. Constantine R.; '*Manipur Maid of Mountains,*' New Delhi, Lancers publishers, 1981, pp. 22-26.
14. Singh, K.B.; '*Social Stratification and Mobility in Manipur,*' p. 62.
15. James Hastings, (eds.), '*Encyclopedia of Religion and Ethics,*' Charles Scribners Sons, New York, vol. 8, 1964, p. 402.
16. Horam, M.; '*Naga Polity,*' Low Price Publications, Delhi, 1992, p. 42.
17. Chandra, M. Singh; '*Panthoibi Khongul,*' Imphal, 1999, p. 32.

18. *Chakpa Khunda Khunthok*, (Both Khaba and Pakhangba had enmity, which is also given in Pakhangba Laihui) M.S. sources, N Khelchandra.
19. Khelchandra N., '*Naothingkhong Phambal Kaba*,' Imphal, 1995, p. 1.
20. *Tutenglon*, M.S.
21. Lizangnee Gangte, Unpublished article on Communal Harmony.
22. Culloch, W.Mc; '*An Account of the valley of Manipur*,' Calcutta.1859, p. 4.
23. Kamei, Gangumei; '*Ethnicity and politics*,' unpublished article presented at the talk programmed on '*Ethnicity and Politics of Manipur*', org. by NRC at M.U. 16 Sept. 2003.
24. Kamei, Gangumei; '*Crisis of Identity*,' Journal of M.U. Research Club, Imphal 1997. p. 147
25. Ibungohal. L.; '*Introduction to Manipur*,' Imphal, 1963, p. 10.
26. *Op.cit.*; '*The Meitheis*.'
27. *Op.cit.*: '*Manipur, Maid of the Mountains*,' p. 31.
28. *Op.cit.* '*The Meitheis*,' p. 11.
29. *Ibid.*, M Horam mentioned in his forwarding portion of '*The Meithei's*,' Delhi. B.R. Publishing Corporation. 1975.

III
Expansion Movement

The British colonial administration and their divide and rule policy had played an important role in the movement of identity expansion. In short, it was responsible for indiscriminately dividing the hill tribes into Naga and Kuki. This classification led to ethnic identification of the tribes into these two constellations. Here it is to be noted from different angles about the changing dichotomy of tribes to ethnic groups would be an evolution of usage in the academic parlance. By tribes we denote groups of people that are in traditional or primitive societies and on the other hand ethnic groups or ethnicity indicate that have develop something with the changing historical discourse rather than in isolation.[1]

However, identification with Naga has been a process of pan-Naga identity. The formation of ethnic identity has the potential to divide the larger social or political groupings along the ethnic lines where it leads to the upheaval in different direction. The ethnic identification of tribes into Naga constellation which may be called a process of Nagaisation has social, cultural and political implications. The issues become more complicated due to the continuing process of identity assertion, formation and expansion movement of the Naga themselves. During the Second World War, R.R. Shimray was surprised when intruding Japanese troops called him Naga, for he thought himself as a Tangkhul, not as a Naga and later it was the local interpreter who told him that the Tangkhul are also Nagas.[2] Alemchiba also expressed similar view that as late as 1954, he found the people of 'Tuensang' rarely speaking of themselves as Nagas but as 'Konyaks,' 'Changs,' 'Phoms' and so on.

This process was greatly strengthened by the Naga insurgency for independence based on the Naga nationalism. From the very beginning, Naga National Council (NNC) movement led by Phizo to get independence of Nagaland, had tried to make Naga nationality and a viable territory of his dream by expanding its territory, which were inhabited in surrounding Naga Hills district of Assam, Manipur, Arunachal Pradesh and across the border. The same political dream and line was followed by NSCN (IM). After 1965, they wanted to get it into practice. So they organised and mobilised the various communities of Manipur hills with the political tone of Naga sovereignty by using anti-Meitei card. Even they used the method of ethnic cleansing in these areas. So Naga-Kuki clash was happened in 90s. After 1996, NSCN (IM) was in the process of peace talk with the government of India in order to get good chances for mobilising the Manipuri Nagas to consolidate and solidify them as Naga oneness by demanding all the Naga inhabited areas under one administrative unit. That's why alteration of Manipur boundary became the central agenda of the peace talk. So the people of this region have been witnessing interaction and reaction between the Manipuri Nagas and Manipuri Meiteis.

Now Nagas are more or less regarded as an emerging marginal nationality. Within the broad Naga constellation, there were several tribal solidarity processes and it is still going on. Among the Tangkhul one of the major Naga tribe of Manipur have dialectical differences for almost every village, but the adoption of Ukhrul dialect as the standard Tangkhul literary language has strengthened the Tangkhul identity and unity. The 'Zemei', 'Liangmei' and 'Rongmei' also started the Zeliangrong movement to forge unity and promote integration among these cognate tribes. A Zeliangrong identity has now been formed. During the post-independence period, the Anal, Moyon, Monsang and Lamkang tribes organised the 'Pakan' movement to bring the four tribes under one common name 'Pakan' but it failed.[4] The Moyon and Monsang tribes tried to combine into 'Mon' but the separate feelings between themselves are still very strong.

Again the Kom-Rem movement was also organised with a view to bring the Kom, Chiru, Aimol, Purum and one time the Koireng to give a common identity to these tribes. The Mao-Maram tribal alliance for political purpose has not led to social or cultural integration. The Poumai group does not like to be grouped with Mao tribe.

Among the Kukis there is no such process of integration till the Mizo insurgency. While Kuki rebellion (1917-1919) was aimed at Kuki 'independence,' it did not lead to further integration but distinguished it into distinct tribes. But the Mizo integration movement again restored a sense of unity among these tribes. The concept of Kuki-Mizo was popularised. Now it is being replaced by 'Zomi' movement after the solution of the Mizo rebellion. The 'Zo' or 'Zomi' identity is again catching on among the Kuki-Chin tribes of Manipur and surrounding areas, though tribal identities have not been submerged under it. The Chin-Kuki-Mizo (CHIKIM) solidarity process is continuing while the Thadou are asserting their Kuki identity.

Changing Dynamics

It is the major tendency of highlanders of Manipur i.e. both the Naga and the Kuki that the people of the same race now scattered under different administrative units have a right to be grouped together and brought under the same administration or administrative unit because they already have such unit in Nagaland and Mizoram. So the Manipuri Nagas want to merge to Nagaland and Manipuri Kukis to Mizoram.[5] These are the dreams of the Nagas and Kukis underground outfits and their frontal organisations. To them it is merely a question of adjusting the state boundaries of Manipur but naturally it is a very painful to the valley people. In short demanding of Mizo south district and south Nagaland in the territory of Manipur means to alter the territorial boundary of Manipur. The popular leaders of the valley including those who were ministers began to say 'you are free to go and join your kinsmen in Nagaland or Mizoram if you want to, but leave the land behind'. Highlanders' answers–' if your king held away over our land by remote control, we have lived on it for centuries. We will continue to live here. Why should we leave our land belong to Nagaland or Mizoram.'[6]

The basic argument of demanding Southern Nagaland and Southern Mizoram district is associated with the movement of Nagas and Mizos independence. No one denied the fact within the paradigm of politicisation of a nation or state formation; basically the masses are heeding to draw a definite political territory as an essential element of state. For such they have need land (viable definite territory) and people (some nationality). Without one of each element, no one could form a state. Among the elements of the state, territory is the root of all. So the fourth world people always try to demarcate their own definite territory if that is not existed or established. But having communal politics and narrow sight, it is always based on racial boundary. It is better to close this chapter because if that goes on why not America is merged to Britain, Kashmir to Pakistan and both be merged to Iran, West Bengal to Bangladesh and why not the people of north east should be merged either to Myanmar or Thailand or China. That would mean escalating unending nation's reorganisation.[7]

The same political formula is being applied by NSCN (IM) and its frontal organisations. One may assess very easily that it is not the clash of civilisation though Huntington emphasis in the contemporary discourse because it is not related with culture, language and religion as civilised identity but it is related with the question of territory. The main factor is majority of NSCN (IM) cadre are from Manipur but they are fighting for the Naga cause i.e. sovereignty of Naga people. The territory is Nagaland, the land which all the Nagas are inhabited. If the success story of their movement either sovereignty or maximum autonomy comes up, the fruit of it will go to Nagaland and its people only, not to Manipuri Nagas. But the Nagas living in Manipur have been compelled to follow suit with the expansion of Nagaland or creation of a new Naga state separated from Manipur i.e. southern Nagaland or South Nagaland.[8] So it needs to see their aspiration in connection with Manipuri Naga and Nagas of Nagaland vis-à-vis Nagas of Manipur with Meiteis.'

In the relationship between Manipuri Meiteis and Manipuri Nagas, merger of Manipuri's Nagas territory with Nagaland has a long story. After independence in 1947, the Manipuri Nagas in Mao which adjoins Nagaland raised this slogan (Naga integration). The movement was led by Athiko Daiho, who later became the Finance Minister in the union territory of Manipur. At the time of demand was put forwarded, Manipur had not merged with the union of India and Nagaland was yet to be a state. It was existed merely as Naga Hills district of Assam. Manipur had a popular ministry in the system of constitutional monarchy with MK Priyobrata Singh as Chief Minister. Those in the Ministry includes Ralengnao Khathing, who later became chief secretary of Nagaland and Indian ambassador to Burma, Khathing, a Tangkhul Naga from erstwhile district of Manipur East was the minister in charge of hill areas. At that time Daiho began a non-tax campaign against the Manipur rulers. There was police firing in one place of the Mao area. Daiho was arrested and put into the jail. The demand was gradually lost its initial momentum.[9] He was later pacified by accommodating him as an advisor of Manipur administration.

It again resurfaced in 1954 when fourteen Naga leaders of Manipur submitted a joint memorandum to the central government making out a firm determination for the regrouping of the Naga areas as one administrative unit. Angal Anal, a congress worker of Tengnoupal with some Naga leaders put up a theory that the Naga hostile were gaining a foothold in the Manipur hills because of the discontentment arising from the valley domination of the hills.[10] According to them merger was the ideal solution for the problem posed by the hostile Nagas. But the union government did not give positive response. As a result of it, the merger issue of Manipuri's Naga inhabiting area to Nagaland was completely faded.

Lois and Highlanders Getting same Faith

The 'Lois' as mentioned earlier in the chapter II, were created out of the Meiteis for their social offences and not born as such originally. Most of them were scattering at different places of Manipur like highlanders and now-a-days they are classified as scheduled castes. They also have their clans and they are the real Meitei who cannot be touched by the religious hands of Vaishnavism. But they cannot be called as Meitei. The canvassing of Meitei to all the inhabitants of Manipur (including seven clans and highlanders) was going up to 18th century. It was carried on the sense that they were unclean because of their habit of meat eating, poultry keeping, piggeries and preparation of wine. These were done only when Meiteis of valley were converted as Vaishnavite communities. Some intellectuals gave their opinion that it might be the Meiteis of all if the Meitei king could finish canvassing Meitei (plural ethnic canvass) before Vaishnavism came.[11]

From the record of history of Manipur, it is clearly given that all the people who inhabited in Manipur are clans of Meiteis. In the course of time, they are treated as Naga and Kuki. It is an undisputed fact that all are from same ancestor so it is better to use the term 'Manipuri Meitei', 'Manipuri Naga' and 'Manipuri Kuki' in order to bring common name to all because it needs moral integration. Moreover we have needed to recall the adorning of tribal dress and to bring the most sacred fire (Andro Mei) at the time of coronation of Meitei King.[12] It indicates the best example of hill-Lois and valley unity. Moreover in 'Lai-Haraoba' (Indigenous festival of the Meitei for appeasing god), it cannot be ended without the scene of Tangkhul.

Crisis of Meitei Identity

It is earlier mentioned that Meitei is composed of seven clans namely Mangang (Ningthouja), Luwang, Khuman, Moirang, Angom, Sarang-Leisangthem, Khaba-Nganba. All of these seven clans were merged to only one nomenclature as 'Meitei'. But the identity of Meitei is a very controversial issue. The cultural revivalism represented by the 'Sanamahi' movement had successfully challenged the notion of Aryan origin of Meitei. This identity confusion emerges because of the multiple ethnic roots of the Meitei nationality.[13] The crisis of Meitei identity began with its entry into religious arena i.e. the atrocious imposition of an alien socio-religious cultural system which had been despotically regulated through repressive measures under fanatical regime having no religious tolerance.[14]

One of the important features of the identity problem of Meitei is that though they were a majority group, they could not bring the hill tribes into their identity expansion canvass. After Sanskritisation, the king had adopted the name of Manipur and Manipuri has been widely used to mean the Meitei peoples and Meitei language only. The hill tribes feel that they were outside the connotation of the terms of Manipuris or Meitei. The process of Christianisation among the hill tribes and Sanskritisation among the Meitei have multiplied more complicacies in their effort to resolve identity crisis. Yet the Meiteis have at best restored their spirit of nationalism despite confronting certain misconceived notion of identity.[15]

Repercussion

Though the consciousness of ethnic identity of tri-ethnic groups is well established, the problems of names remain complex as ever before. The hill tribes do not call them Manipuri's nor the Meitei call them as such. The tribes prefer to call themselves as Nagas or Kuki or Mizo or by their tribe names though Manipuri means the Meitei people or Manipuri language, a section of Meitei or Meetei. Majority of the Meitei revivalist, who want to revive Sanamahism (indigenous religion) do not have intention to call them Manipuri because this is the name given by the outsider. If this tendency continues, it will logically lead to a situation where Manipuri may become just a mere geographical expression. So it depends on the willingness of the people inhabiting in both hill and valley.

The cleavages among tri-ethnic groups of Manipur were done by the external forces in the past. They were both religions-Sanskritisation and Christianisation, British colonialism and the present administration that followed the same pattern of colonial legacy. The Christian missionaries played an important role which imparted western education along with missionary activities and created a strong sense of consciousness among the hill tribes. At the time of their arrival, the colonial authorities divided their areas of activities not on the basis of north-south, east-west but on the basis of Naga areas and Kuki areas led by William Pettigrew 'American Baptist mission' and Watkins Robert 'North-East India General

Mission' earlier known as 'Thadou Kuki Pioneer Mission' respectively.[16] But no one cared about these external forces, instead of it some misguided-elements had feeding irrelevant arguments and wrote a new history without facts. Thus Rajat Kanti Das rightly observes that 'the Marings, one of the Nagas tribe of Manipur were motivated to call themselves Naga more by the Church leaders than by any other agency.'[17]

The emergence of ethnic nationalism instead of having Manipuri nationalism compounded and confused the social fabrics of Manipur. These ethnic identities become so pervasive and people become willing to die for their nation,[18] particularly for their respective ethnic community but not for the majority interests. As consequence the people of hill and valley are in the process of assertion of interest of each group and reaction of it. So Manipur becomes breeding ground of conflicts and it could also turn as conundrum without delay. That's why different people are tried to see and examine such volatile situation of this region.

If we are going to analyse all together, it will be realised that the major issue is concerned with the construction of identity and its territorial dimension. That is why the question of identity crisis and its political implication is arising. One may give the proper answer of it by stating that ethnic consolidation in Manipur is the gift of participant political culture in our democracy. As stated earlier, the involvement of some section of the tribes in the Naga movement from the early part of independence period, have encouraged and motivated to identify themselves as Nagas at the social level.

The same process is going on in the 1990s with overtone of fearness by the ethnic feuds. Now-a-days a good numbers of Kuki tribes in Manipur such as the Monsang, Anal, Moyon, Lamkang, Chothe, Chiru, and Kom were identified as Naga, their migration from parts of Chin Hills of Myanmar and their being closer to Mizo-Kuki-Chin group both culturally and linguistically notwithstanding.[19] This process of Nagaisation of the tribes to come under one fold or identified with the term 'Naga' is linked to the kind of power structure where the state has come to experience a democratic political set-up in which democratic institution is there but democratic politics is not existing at all. These are by products of immature and confusion nationalism of various ethnic groups. Therefore, the present crisis in Manipur is associated with identity and its political implications.

Notes and References

1. See Eriksen TH; '*Ethnicity & Nationalism;*' Pluto press, London, 1993.
2. Shimray, R.R.; '*Origin and Culture of Nagas,*' New Delhi, Somsok Publications, 1985, p. 39.

3. Alemchiba, M.; 'A *Historical Account of Nagaland*,' Naga Institute of Culture, Kohima, p. 24.
4. Johnson Anal, W.S.; '*The Pakan Tribes of Manipur*,' The Anal Naga Student's Union, Manipur, 1994, p. 3.
5. Aide-memoir to the Prime Minister of India for immediate creation of Kukiland, submitted by Kuki National Front (KNF) on 8 April 1998.
6. *The Freedom*, Imphal, 8 Dec., 1993.
7. Dhanabir Laishram; '*North East in Benthic Zone*,' Akansha Publishing House, New Delhi 2007, p. 153.
8. Interview with Pabung Iboyaima, dt. 6. April, 2007.
9. Constantine, R.; '*Manipur Maid of Mountain*,' New Delhi, Lancers Publishers, 1981, p. 129.
10. *Ibid*.
11. Personal interview with L.S. Guite; dt.22 August, 2004.
12. It was used to lighting a lamp for the coronation of the king.
13. Kamei, Gangumei; 'Crisis of identity in Manipur,' *Journal of MU Research Club*, Imphal, 1997, p. 150.
14. Indrakumar, H.; '*Basic Dimension of Identity and Integration; A Critical appraisal on Meitei Perspective*,' Imphal, 2002, p. 7.
15. *Ibid*., p. 42.
16. *Sanathong*, Monthly Journal, Imphal, June 2004, vol. 10, Issue.4.
17. Pakem, B. (eds.) '*Nationality, Ethnicity and Cultural Identity in North East India*,' Omsons Publications, Guwahati, 1990, p. 246.
18. See Benedict A.; '*Imagined Communities*,' Verso, London, 1991.
19. Op.cit.

IV
Demanding Homeland

Before the advent of the British to the region, the Nagas were unknown to the rest of the world. The modern sense of the nation state or independence was not known to them but every Naga village has been a republic having its own village government and each village was being socially self-sufficient.[1] The emergence of common ethnic identity consciousness of the Nagas was a gift of British colonialism as they grouped the tribes under a generic name for the convenience in administration and ethnographic purposes. The First World War had exposed Nagas to the outside world. The American Baptist missionaries spread Christianity imparting education and other western culture to these people. It was through this education where Nagas open up a new chapter of their social and political consciousness.

Their exposure to the outside world had formed the consciousness of ethnicity as it becomes an organised movement after the return of Labour Corps which served during the First World War. It formed the Naga Club with some Christian educated government officials and a number of headmen from around the two principle villages of Kohima and Makokchung in 1918. The chief concern of this organisation was about the political future of the Nagas. This was the turning point in the political history of Nagas. This organisation submitted a memorandum to the British 'India Statutory Commission' popularly known as 'Simon Commission' on January 10, 1929 that the Nagas would become free as 'they have been before,' when the British leave and the future of the Nagas could never be bound by any arbitrary decisions of the British government.[2]

In 1945, at the initiative of Charles Pawsey, the then deputy commissioner, the Naga Hills District Tribal Council (NHDTC) was formed with a primary objective to unite the Naga areas on the modern lines. In the next year the name was changed to Naga National Council (NNC). At that time the political objective of NNC was local autonomy for the hills within the province of Assam and training of Nagas for self-government. In 1947, as Independence approached, Naga leaders submitted a memorandum to the last Governor General Lord Mountbatten, suggesting that India might act as a guardian power for ten years only after which the Naga people would be free to determine their political future. On 20th May 1947, when a sub-committee of the advisory committee on aboriginal tribes visited Kohima, the Naga leaders reiterated the same view.

In a further development Sir Akbar Hydari, the then governor of Assam with the leaders of the Naga National Council signed an agreement comprising of nine points, at Kohima. By this agreement the right of the Nagas to develop themselves according to their wishes was recognised. But the article 9th of the agreement was vaguely worded and proved most controversial one which stated that 'the Governor of Assam as agent of the government of Indian union will have special responsibility for a period of ten (10) years to ensure the due observance of this agreement; at the end of this period the Naga National Council will be asked whether they require the above agreement to be extended for a further period or a new agreement regarding the future of Naga people be arrived at.' It has been interpreted in many ways. The Nagas interpreted that they had the right to claim independence after a period of ten years. To the government, it means that after ten years same agreement may be renewed or a fresh agreement may be arrived at. The interpretation of the same article in different angles formed the bottom line of the Naga issue.

Akbar Hydari, the signatory representing the government of India warned the Nagas that if Naga Hills District, in fact, refused to join the Indian union, it would use force against them. But the Naga people regard that the agreement have the liberty to demand complete separation. So on 19th July 1947, a Naga delegation under the leadership of Phizo met Mahatma Gandhi at Bhangi colony, New Delhi and confirmed the declaration of Naga independence though they had no agreement with the government of India.[3]

To pursue their aspiration, NNC declared Naga independence on 14th August, 1947 when they realised that the Constituent Assembly of India had backtracked on the nine point agreement and ignored the provision. But NNC, in fact, was not unanimous on the issue of Naga independence before, during and even after the declaration of Naga independence.[4] There emerged two groups in the NNC where one group wanted to remain within the Indian union whereas another group led by A.Z. Phizo who did not accept the Hydari agreement as they thought the terms of the agreement were sort of self-determination for Nagas.

After Phizo became the president of Naga National Council in the early part of 1950s, Naga nationalism gained momentum and was accelerated. In May 1951, he organised a 'Plebiscite' in which thousands of Nagas gave their thumb impressions in favour of independence. In the meantime the first general election of independent India was to take place. Naga nationalists' showed non-acceptance of the Indian Constitution and its Sixth Schedule. Not a single voter of Naga turned up to this first election of Nagaland though the government of India went through the whole process of preparing electoral rolls, calling for nominations and setting up polling booths. It was a total boycott of the election, no one filed nomination and not a single voter turned up. During these days underground movement in Nagaland became extremely active.

In March 1956 the underground Naga Federal Government was formed. There was an underground Parliament called 'Tatar Hoho,' and organisation of Home Guards with a Commander in Chief, and a Council of Kilonsers (Ministers) with an Ato Kilonser (Prime-Minister). The President of the Federal Government was called Kedaghe. From 1956 to 1958, Nagaland witnessed large scale violence in action and armed forces moved in. Seeing that violence causing in a worsen situation, the Naga Peace Organising Committee (NPOC) was formed in 1956. Then a Naga People's Convention (NPC) was called. In May 1958, the second Naga Peoples Convention was held at Ungma. A liaison committee was appointed to contact the underground with a view to bring about a political settlement. In October 1959, the third NPC was held at Mokokchung and it was decided to propose that Nagaland might be made into a separate state within the Indian Union and the Ministry of External Affairs.[5]

In July 1960, the then Prime Minister Nehru and Naga delegation reached 16 point agreement. Consequently, on 1st August 1960, Prime Minister Nehru announced the decision of the government in Parliament to make Nagaland the sixteenth state of the Indian Union. Subsequently, an interim body was set up and after the due preparation Nagaland state was inaugurated on 13th December, 1963 by the then President Dr. Radhakrishnan. After 1963, it becomes a triangular situation in which the two major parties were—the Naga underground and the Nagaland state Government, and the third party being the Government of India. The underground Naga organisations remain in the soil of Nagaland. The Naga territorial integration or expansion of southern Nagaland was also not taken place. It was really the same case of missing the bus to the Manipuri Nagas leaders who wanted to integrate all the Naga inhabited areas of Manipur under one single administrative unit of Nagaland.[6]

The situation turned to worse in the first half of 1970s. Several underground groups were gone to China for training in guerilla warfare. A spate of violence was witnessed throughout the state. In the General Election of 1974, eighteen human lives were lost. The Government launched massive crackdown on insurgents. But peace at last returned to Nagaland in the last quarter of 1975, when the underground leaders took the initiative for peace talks which culminated in the historic Shillong Accord of 11th November 1975 whereby the underground of their own volition, accepted the Indian Constitution and agreed to lay down the arms held by their men. Action under the Unlawful Activities (Prevention) Act, by virtue of which the underground organisations, 'Nagaland National Council' 'Federal Government of Nagaland (FGN)' and 'Naga Federal Army (NFA)' had been outlawed, was suspended and the erstwhile rebels came over-ground and joined their families to lead a peaceful life as citizens of India. The decision of the rebels to bid farewell to arms, may or may not have been motivated by a genuine change of heart, but there is no doubt that the major factor responsible to the changed stance of the underground was the altered situation of Nagaland in the last preceding four years.[7]

During this period the state had all round progress in all fronts. Zashie Huire and Biseto Medom became President and Home Minister of the Nagaland Federal

Government respectively and were quickly to realise that the underground movement was petering out and there was no hope of keeping it alive for long in view of the mass surrenders and captures of the rebels. So they took the initiative for the peace talks and signed the Shillong Accord.[8]

The Shillong Peace Accord was primarily responsible for the change of democratic process in the election of the state. In 1978 Assembly election, there was record of 80 to 85 per cent voters turned out at various polling booths to elect their representatives to the state Assembly. It ignored the faint boycott call given by a section of misguided elements in what remained of the Naga underground movement. The popular enthusiasm in the electoral process was equally shared by a large number of erstwhile underground leaders and members; and people not only enrolled themselves as voters but also took active interest in the battle of ballot. But Phizo, who settled down in England following his escape from the Naga Hills in the late sixties, was quick to repudiate the agreement. Muivah, the pro-Peking General Secretary of NNC, the political arm of the underground who had been camping along with his China trained groups in the lightly administered Kachin Hills of Burma (now Myanmar) adjoining Nagaland, too rejected the accord.[9] So the issue of southern Nagaland could not be beyond the question. Still the common political aspiration of Manipuri Nagas and Nagas of Nagaland are in different direction. It may be realised that the underground factions of NSCN have different views and set of ideas. The vivid example is the incidents of Kohima and Dimapur in 1995. Povezo Soho, deputy commander-in-chief of the federal government of Nagaland was allegedly assassinated by NSCN (IM) in 1995. Enraged by it, the Chakesang in Phek district of Nagaland issued a quit notice on Tangkhuls in Phek and NSCN (IM) responded with a death sentence on those who signed the quit notice.[10] Further as many as 21 Tangkhuls were killed in Kohima and Dimapur by unidentified gunmen during the period from 8 May 1995 to 6 June 1998.[11]

Different Aspiration of Manipuri Nagas

During that time tribal leaders of Manipur—A Daiho, Thangkopao Kipgen, F.F. Pearson, Suisa, Tiankham and Teba Kilong were busy in drafting Manipur State Constitution Act 1947 and Hill Area Regulation Act. These leaders were important members of the constitution making body and drafting sub-committee. They had not the tendency of Naga integration in spite of their educational qualification and prevailing condition of Nagaland. The Manipuri Nagas were not taking part in the 'Naga plebiscite' of May 16, 1951 which was carried out only in the Naga Hills, an administrative unit within the state of Assam.[12] In the first Lok Sabha Election of 1952, three Naga political parties were contested. They were Mao Maram Union (MMU), Manipur Zeliangrong Union (MZU) and Naga National League (NNL) of Manipur. Also in the election of 1957, Congress Party (National Party) got the outer Manipur Constituency. The Congress candidate defeated not only the socialist candidate but also four independent candidates in the outer Manipur constituency.[13]

After the Daiho was shrinking from Naga integration movement, its leadership was taken over by Romeo, the Manipuri Tangkhul Naga. He later joined the hostiles in Nagaland and occupied important position in the 'Federal Government.' He belongs to the due Manipur Naga Council (MNC), a branch of the Naga National Council of Nagaland. By 1975, Romeo became the Chief spokesman of the merger move. The MNC called for the boycott of the 1962 parliament poll, but the Nagas in the Manipur hills casted their vote just for the same. Disillusioned with the failure of their boycott call, most of the leaders of the MNC joined the hostiles. This spelt the doom of the integration movement. With hostiles taking up the issue, it got inextricably mixed up with their demand for independence for the Nagas. Nothing more was needed to make the merger demand, take on anti-national hues and thus losing what democratic luster it had. Rishang Keishing,[14] the Tangkhul Naga leader of Manipur who represented outer Manipur in the 1952-57 Lok Sabha (LS) and then again from 1962-67, opposed the inclusion of Manipur areas to Nagaland under the circumstances then prevailing in the later state. The situation in Nagaland was not very reassuring and it was a very real threat to national integration. In that situation Manipur Naga areas merging with Nagaland would mean throwing in their lot with a disturbed area. So, as long as national territorial integrity was endangered in Nagaland, it would be highly unwise to bring all the Nagas in the north-east into the state of Nagaland.[15]

But after his defeat (Rishang) in 1967 General Elections, he formed the Naga Integration Committee and took up the merger agitation in a big way. Whatever might have been his motivations, the situation in which he took over the leadership of the merger movement was qualitatively different from that which dissuaded him from lending its support earlier. But not all the Nagas in Manipur are keen about joining Nagaland. They are afraid that in an integrated Nagaland, they will be hard to put to come into their own. For example in the matter of jobs the Nagas enjoy rights by reservations. In a consolidated Naga political unit like Nagaland, this right will not be theirs any more. The whole state being that of scheduled tribes, the Manipur Nagas will have to take equal chances with the rest of them. Not only the above point of their advantages in job, Manipuri Nagas also do not like to strain the long blood relationship of hill and valley from the same ancestor, having common historical background and inter-economic dependency of each other's.[16]

In connection with above propositions, mention may be made of some interesting evidence where the hill people had objected the demand of greater Nagaland or so called southern Nagaland. Manipuri Nagas were only people who reacted against the government of Nagaland when they tried to set up water supply project in the Zhuko River. Manipuri Naga stated that Nagaland Government could not take a single drop of water of Manipur. If they did so, bloodshed should be the last decision.[17] Then another incident was happened in Mao area when the government of Nagaland constructed a T.B. Hospital by encroaching in a little portion of Manipur's boundary. At that time, Manipuri Mao Nagas broke down the hospital. Again in the Ukhrul district, one of the strongholds of the Naga integration movement, there is still the boundary issue between Jessami and its adjoining areas of Nagaland where it could lead to internecine killings amongst the Nagas tribe.

Kukis for Kuki Homeland

Kuki-Chin group of people lived in this place since ancient period. Although this same group of people was known in different names as 'Chin' in Myanmar and Kuki or Mizo or Lushai in India, Meitei called them as Khongsai. It is argued that they came to Manipur only between 16th to 19th century from Chin Hills of Burma (Myanmar) to Manipur. Although it is said the kingdom of Manipur had a larger area in the olden days than the one at present, where it covered the portions of Burma into Ningthi River in the east and in the south it was extended beyond Chin Hills up to the sea.[18] It is interesting that the word 'Naga' was given by the outsiders became a cementing force to the varied tribes despite their extreme heterogeneity and cut throat hegemony but in the case of Kukis, it appears to be a division in unity. Linguistically, unlike the Nagas, they can communicate to one another with the least effort in their respective dialects.

Their dreams of an organised entity appeared for the first time with the formation of Kuki National Assembly (KNA) in 1946.[19] It was the apex social organisation that spearheaded the issues relating to the interest of the Kukis in the early part of independence of India. In its general assembly held at Thingkangphai, then Manipur south district, KNA passed a resolution to create a 'Kuki state' and send a representation to the Prime Minister, Nehru.[20] As an offshoot of the Naga unrest in the Naga Hills and offspring of the Mizo rebellion in Mizo hills, towards the beginning of 1965, the Kukis of Manipur and their cousins, Lushai of Mizo hills held a conference at Churachandpur to discuss about their political future. One group wanted to demand a sovereign state for the Kukis and Lushai of Manipur and Assam known as Mizoram whereas another group wanted Mizoram but as a state within the Indian Union. The later outnumbered the former and the members of the conference pulled themselves apart.[21] In January 1966, KNA met near Imphal and passed a resolution to uphold the unity and territorial integrity of the tribe within Manipur. But the supporters of the independent Mizoram in Manipur, who were sulking after the setback they had suffered in Churachandpur the year before took hard and joined the Mizo rebels. Thus with a well-defined political motives, the Kukis began enhancing their struggle to achieve their asserted interest.

The people of North East witnessed the vibrant activities of Mizos armed struggle in the mid-sixties. It was the Mizo National Front (MNF) under the leadership of Laldenga, who led an armed struggle for a sovereign state of Mizos. Demkhosit Gangte, who was one of the delegates of KNA in the Mizo People's Convention (MPC) at Kawnpui in 1965, joined hands with Laldenga. Thereby the KNA-MNF axis was established in the struggle for the common cause to secure a sovereign state for the Mizos.

In their armed struggle for creation of a separate state for all the Kukis and the Mizos who were scattered under different administrative units, passed a resolution for creation of a state on 14th April 1971.[22] It said 'to put all Mizo tribes including those living in our neighborhood under one set up of administration, the house consider lasting peace and tranquility and statehood as of imperative necessity and decided to bring this to the notice of the central government as soon as possible.' It was done in reaffirmation of the decision taken earlier at Kawnpui convention to create an administrative unit so as to build up territorial integrity of the areas inhabited by the Kuki-Chin-Mizo. On the eve of signing the Mizo Accord in which their movement was pacified by granting a new state of Mizoram, Laldenga in his statement appeared in the *Times of India* on 8 May 1985, claimed that 'the Government of India has agreed the inclusion of Kuki/Hmar inhabited areas to the newly created state of Mizoram and further claimed that a large chunk of Manipur territory contiguous to Mizoram will be merged with the state.'

In August 1987, there emerged Kuki National Organization (KNO) with its constituent Kuki

National Army (KNA) demanding an autonomous state for the Kukis in Sakiang division of Myanmar. Another section wanted a Kuki homeland, comprised parts of Ukhrul, Senapati, Churachandpur and Imphal valley (including Imphal and Bishnupur) and Kuki inhabited areas of Assam and Nagaland. On 18 May 1988, Nehlun Kipgen also founded the Kuki National Front (KNF) at Molnoi with the objective for the continuation of demand for Kukiland.[23] According to T.S. Gangte, the said front was established to accelerate the demand earlier raised by the Kuki National Assembly for creating Kukiland and also to defend the Kukis from the atrocities and brutalities of the anti-national Naga activists. The Kukiland demanded by KNF consisted of the districts of Churachandpur, Chandel, parts of Tamenglong and Senapati. Another armed Kuki ethnic outfits, Kuki National Army (KNA) active in Manipur and Myanmar also claimed these areas as the constituents of Zale'ngam or the Kuki nation.[24]

But Manipuri Nagas and Manipuri Kukis are not in favour of such claims. All such claims and demands are inter-related with each other and they also realised that it was only the handiwork of India to alter the boundary of Manipur in order to aggravate voluminous internal contradiction.[25] Still the Government fermented the issues and remain unresolved. The main issue of internal contradiction in between Naga underground vis a vis Kuki and Meetei and Naga people is associated with different political aspiration and vested interest of their leaders.

The different tribes of Nagaland such as Konyaks, Aos, Semas, Angamis, Chakesangs, Changs, Lothas, Phoms, Sangtams, Yamchungers, Zeliangs etc. are different from each other as the Mao, Tangkhul and Kabui Nagas of Manipur. In Nagaland, pidgin Assamese locally known as Nagamese is the inter-tribal language of communication. In the remote interior areas even Nagamese is not understood. The same case is done in Manipur also. The different tribes of Manipur do not also understand each other's languages. Even among the sub-tribes, one village does not understand the language of another two miles away.[26] But in case of Kuki-Chin groups, they can at least communicate in their own respective dialects.

According to L. Solomon, the Naga leader who was finance minister in the former union territory of Manipur, the language in which they can communicate each other in the state is Manipuri. Ninety per cent of the Naga tribes are fluent in this language. That is why Nagamese of Nagaland is utterly foreign to the Manipuri Nagas. It is quite right to say that major obstacle in Naga solidarity has been the diversity of the Naga dialects, there being as many dialects as there are tribes and even being sub-tribes from village to village within a single tribe.[27] English and pidgin Assamese (Nagamese) are the inter-tribal language or language of inter communication in Nagaland. Like the same way, the highlanders of Manipur are using Manipuri and English as inter-tribal language of communication. Therefore, Manipuri language is the only language which tries to integrate the tri-ethnic groups of Manipur because common language is the most important element of unity.

Even in customs and habits, the Nagas are not one. The Maram tribe in north district of Manipur does not eat pork. For the rest of the Naga community, pork is considered the main cuisine of any festive meal. Among the Tangkhul, who are one solid bloc among the Manipuri Naga tribes, there are the people who eat beef and buffalo meat and those who consider it altogether it as taboo. Moreover in Manipur hill, the creation of enmity between the Naga and Kuki is happening since the beginning of 19th century. They seem to have the attitude of vengeance in both the movements of highlanders such as Kuki rebellion and Jadonang movement etc. Even there were bloodsheds in the hill areas due to having high enmity and led to ethnic clash between 1993 to 1997. But in Nagaland such enmity among the different tribes was not happened except driven out of Manipuri Tangkhuls from Nagaland.

Notes and References

1. Singh, K.S.; *'Tribal movement in India,'* vol. 1. New Delhi, Manohar Publications, 1982, p. 41.
2. V. Sumi and K. Timothy, *'Cry for Justice,'* (MIP, GPRN) date and place of publication not cited. p. 178.
3. Sarin, V.K.; *'India's North East in Flames,'* New Delhi, Vikas Publishing House, 1981, p. 97.
4. Vashum, R.; *'Nagas Right to Self-determination; An Anthropological-historical Perspective,'* New Delhi, Mittal Publications, 2000, p. 73.
5. Nuh, V.K. (Compiled) and Lasuh, Wetshokhrolo (Ed), *'The Naga Chronicle,'* New Delhi, Regency Publications, 2002, p. 27.
6. A process of attempting to consolidate the Naga ethnic identity has been on forcefully after India gained its independence, and more so after Manipur became democratic state. This process has been marked by a flurry of activities-writing Naga history, constructing primordialism of Naga tribes. Influenced by NNC, some tribal leaders in Manipur had started involving in the 'Naga movement' with the formation of the Manipuri Naga Council (MNC) in 1960. Inspite of having such active organisation in Manipur, the Manipuri Naga inhabited areas could not be included in the full-fledged state of Nagaland because people are not interested and even argue with the Nagas of Nagaland because of their treatment to them as Kacha Nagas.
7. *Op. Cit., 'Naga Chronicle.'*

8. *Ibid.*
9. Constantine, R.; '*Manipur Maid of the Mountain,*' New Delhi, Lancers publishers, 1981, pp. 129-30.
10. Bhergese; '*India's North East Resurgent,*' cited from Debashist Mitra, A *setback to NSCN (IM)*, Nagaland newsletter from Kohima, *Statesman*; New Delhi, October, 6, 1995, p. 313.
11. '*A brief report of the UNC for the year 1995-1998,*' UNC Manipur, 1998.
12. Dolly Kikon; '*Carnival of nationalism from the north-east frontiers of India; interpreting Naga nationalism, questioning Indian autonomy and three suggestions for the Indo-Naga peace talks,*' Research paper for the second international conference on Regional Autonomy and Ethnic Minorities: June 10-13, 2004, Uppsala, Sweden.
13. Singh, R.P.; '*Electoral Politics in Manipur,*' New Delhi, Concept Publishing Company, 1981, p. 27.
14. The former Chief Minister and also one of the longest serving Chief Ministers in the political history of Manipur. It indicates that there is no communal politics in Manipur. If one accesses the seat ratio of hill and valley, it is 20:40. Even the minority Muslim could occupy Chief Minister of Manipur. He was Md. Alimuddin. But in case of Naga political elites, they always remain quite about the Naga integration issues whenever they won the election but they were at stake when they lost.
15. *Op. Cit.* '*Manipur: Maid of the Mountains,*' p. 13.

16. Interview with Ito Tongbram on 9 April 2007. He was the Camp Director of Committee for Peace and Integrity (COFPAI) campaign during the Naga-Kuki clashes of 90s.
17. Seminar paper on '*Land Reforms and Ethnic Crisis in North East India*' held on 27th and 28th July 2005, organised by MAKAIAS & History Department, M.U.
18. Roy, Jyotirmoy; '*History of Manipur,*' Calcutta, Eastlight Publishing House, 1973, p. 2.
19. Dena, Lal; '*The Kuki-Naga conflict: Juxtaposed in the colonial context*' in K SAggarwal,(eds.) '*Dynamics of identity and inter-group relations in NE India,*' Simla, Indian Institute of Advanced Study, 1999, p. 186.
20. Gangte, T.S.; '*Land problem and ethnic tension N.E. India with special reference to Manipur,*' paper presented in the national seminar '*Land problem and ethnic crisis in N.E. India*', dated 27th and 28th July 2005.org. by MAKAIAS, Kolkata and Dept. of History, M.U.
21. Op.cit, '*Manipur: Maid of the Mountains,*' p. 66.
22. Aide-memoir to the Prime Minister of India for immediate creation of Kukiland, submitted by Kuki National Front (KNF) on 8 April 1998.
23. *Ibid.*
24. Personal interview with T.S. Gangte, dt. 27 July 2005.
25. *Ibid.*
26. *The freedom*, Imphal, December, 1993.
27. *Ibid.*

V
Self-Determination

The demand for the right to self-determination, which means secession from the Indian union or greater internal autonomy, is the main ideological basis of the present conflict in Manipur. Their logic and discontentment which distorted the common political aspiration of North East India in general and particularly in Manipur are the creation of ethnic states may have satisfied the bigger communities such as Assam for the Assames, Arunachal for the Arunachalis, Nagaland for the Nagas, and Mizoram for the Mizos. But it failed to accommodate the smaller communities and tribes which remained embedded within the larger ethnic groupings of the respective states where all contain a multi-ethnic constellation of populations. Ironically, the existing democratic system primarily function through the representatives of majority population located within a politico-administrative territory in a state. The wishes and aspirations of the minority communities are often ignored and they find themselves completely marginalised where they do not form a majority.[1]

Moreover, state boundaries have been drawn up in such a way that they often cut through the socio-cultural boundaries of certain communities, destroying their natural habitation. The plight of the Kuki-Chin tribes scattered in contiguous states of Assam, Mizoram and Manipur and across the Chin state of Myanmar, the Nagas separated between India's Nagaland and Western Myanmar are the result of this artificial divisions. The complete marginalisation of the indigenous communities through relentless influx of more organised immigrant communities like Bengali and Nepali is also another terrible story. Naturally, most of these communities have resorted to arms to secure their homeland when they realised the little chances to retain control over the resources, or at least ensured their share of it within the areas where they became minority.[2] The same views are in the minds of ethnic minority in Manipur mainly to the Kukis and Nagas.

In the early days of their struggle, most of their ethnic outfits were fought against the structural injustice. But in the later part, it was quite based on relative deprivation theory. Within that periphery comes up with rational choice theory of leader. In a democratic set up, self-determination is a basic right which gives a group independent statehood or expanded power within a federal state. Some scholars have classified self-determination into various types. According to Renon, self-determination is classified into five types such as:

(i) National self-determination, the aspiration to rule one's self and not to be ruled or controlled by others;
(ii) Class self-determination, meaning the proletariat's quest for self-determination to establish the true communist society free from bourgeois exploitation;
(iii) Minorities self-determination, meaning minority should not be forced under any sovereignty which it does not wish to live but be given a fair chance to decide whether it desires to live in an existing sovereignty state or to set up new independent state;
(iv) Racial self-determination meaning the aspiration of people for self-rule on the basis of race and;
(v) Ethnic self-determination, which means that ethnic groups should freely determine the forms of government which ranges from limited autonomy to independence.

Renon himself admits of the inaccuracy of this classification and the minority and ethnic self-determination could better be grouped as one under which racial self-determination may also come. Some other scholars are more inclined to broadly classify the right of self-determination into two—external self-determination and internal self-determination.[3]

External Self-Determination

The classification of self-determination into two is interrelated with the meaning of sovereignty because it has two important elements, internally supreme and externally independent. It means the creation of an independent state or integration of self-determining people with an independent state. In other words, the external self-determination also means separation of self-determining people from an existing state or country of which they are a part to set up a new independent state. According to R.N. Ismagilova, it is meant to fight against relics of colonialism, neo-colonialism and the achievement of state sovereignty. In other words, it is the struggle for a settlement of relations with neighbouring states, land and peoples. The external self-determination thus seems to inbreed secession. External self-determination is practicable during the cold war period because each of the superpower tries to get more and more members in their block. But in the post-cold war period, in this unipolar international politics internal self-determination is projected to minimise violent activities in the world.[4]

Internal Self-Determination

The internal self-determination primarily relates to self-government with a certain degree of autonomy within the boundaries of an existing nation-state. It means the right of people to determine their own social, economic and political system, to utilise their resources and to create environment for their own development within and existing state. In other words, the internal self-determination refers to the autonomy and entity in its political decision making process. It refers to independence of action on the internal or domestic level while foreign affairs and defence are in the hands of the central or national government. The Sami homeland in Finland, the Greenland home rule in Denmark, the Nunavut self-government in Canada and the Kuna autonomy arrangement in Panama are good examples of the implementation of the internal self-determination.[5]

Today, in armed conflict situation of North-east internal self-determination becomes official projection of India to implement through various mechanisms and arrangements within the framework of a nation state and tried to pose up it as ultimately a powerful tool for genuine democracy and federalism.[6] Different armed groups of North-east are in the process of internal self-determination. Major outfits of the region are in the process of peace talks with the Government of India is also the best example of it. But some are still demanding external self-determination and it leads to internal contradiction among themselves.

It becomes autonomy at stake as some are fighting for expansion of territory or creation of a new state within the nation and some are for national liberation (sovereignty). They are in conflicts on the same demand of self-determination as masses have to determine their political, economic and social status. In other words external self-determination is closer with complete independence, but on the other hand, granting of autonomy and creating of a new state or expansion of existing state's territory are within the frame work of internal self-determination. So, good numbers of ethnic armies are being formed in Manipur to protect their ethnic groups and asserting their interest only. At present these are being practised by Kuki militants. They are the by-product of ethnic clashes between Naga and Kuki during 1993-1997.[7] The demand of Kuki homeland and expansion of Mizoram are not burning issues in Manipur. These are the counter proposition of Naga factor and to bargain with the Meitei to understand their position and stand. For them, the problem is mushrooming of ethnic army and possession of ethnic nationalism. These are the views of political implication in the discourse of Identity crisis.[8]

The same views are in the mind of ethnic minority in Manipur mainly to the Kukis and Nagas. Among them, Kukis were being treated as foreigners by the Nagas, so they launched ethnic cleansing by the Nagas militant against the Kukis. But Kukis denied to be foreigners on the ground that they were subjects of the Manipuri kingdom who were settled in the areas of Kabow Valley. After handing over this area to the Myanmar by the first Prime Minister Nehru, they became foreigners. They had faced the problem of migration of population, so they could settle in any part of Manipur and no one could restrain them. From that point of view, they defended the attack of Nagas ethnic cleansing in 1990s. In short logic behind the ethnic nationalism and ethnic armies could be justified by them but they have different demands and aspirations. This is also a part of making confusion for the demanding of self-determination.

The same case happened to both the movements launched by Nagas and Kukis. In the case of Naga's movement, Shillong Accord 1975 was opposed by NSCN. It was formed on 31st January 1980 by Issak Chisi Swu, Thuingaleng Muivah and S.S. Khaplang.

Since then it has been carrying an armed struggle to bring end of Indian colonialism over the Naga people and establish a People's Republic of Nagaland. The Indian Government's persistent efforts to start a dialogue process created differences among the leadership of NSCN and this disagreement took its toll on the organisation. On 30th April 1988, after an attempt to assassinate Muivah failed and in which several cadres were killed, the NSCN splited into two factions, namely the NSCN (K) led by S.S. Khaplang, and the NSCN (IM) led by Isaac and Muivah. The former suspected Isaac and Muivah of secretly initiating talks with the Indian Government.[9]

Now-a-days, all the factions of NSCN have their base areas in Myanmar and training camps in the Chittagong Hills of Bangladesh and Arakan and some parts of Somara Hills of Myanmar. They have links with the Karen and Kachin rebels of Myanmar and also with the ULFA and Bodo rebels. But that is not cordial after it claimed directly greater Nagaland by embracing the surrounding areas from Manipur, Assam and Arunachal Pradesh.[10] Today, these factions of NSCN are in the process of peace talks with the Government of India by demanding maximum autonomy with greater Nagaland and the Kuki militants are also in the process of S.o.O (Suspension of Operation) with the Indian army. The Indo-Naga peace talks have been started since 1997 yet there is no amicable solution between the two parties. Instead both the hill and valley people of Manipur are creating more and more enmity because of governmental initiatives for peace.[11] The following pattern are emerges from governmental initiatives for peace in the North-east:

i) Un-conditional denial of the demand for complete sovereignty or the right to self-determination.
ii) Using developmental initiative for particular schemes to create the context of peace has been a constant theme in the Centre policy on conflict resolution in the North-east. Since 1996, billions of ₹ have been announced as special packages for the North-east.
iii) Poor implementation of each and every government programmes, including the special packages continues to create beneficiaries of conflict.
iv) Surrender of a section of militants and another section continuing to flee.
v) Breaking of existing states and re-organisation of States.[12]

From this initiative for peace in North-eastern states, it is realised that using developmental initiative to create the context of peace as a constant theme and for negotiating with underground organisations; there is possibility of altering the existing boundary of the state. It seems that the gun fighting between the underground militants and the security forces will be stopped but it invites fighting among the various communities. In other words, breaking of existing states and re-organisation of states should lead enmity among the various ethnic groups. That is why the issue of Southern Nagaland is fermented since last 60 years.

Towards an Unbound Dream

It would be a profound error to allow the significance of geographical dimensions or statistics of population or complexities of religion and tribes to the integrated Manipur of the past. Hinduism, Sanamahism, Islam and Christianity all of them have played their important role in the socio-political development of Manipur. All the ethnic groups do not need to hide the force of religion in the structural work of society and their politics. They do not have common religion but have developed common traits of character and have common economic and cultural interests. The ethnic clash among them is a recent development and is the outcome of manipulation by interested politicians and underground groups.[13] Besides, what important is in the formation of an integrated Manipur is not mere social relationship like race, languages and religion but a common memory of the past and the common ideals in the future. That is why the common masses of both hill and valley do not try to fade the spiritual bond of unity where except a few handfuls of political and underground leaders and their frontal organisations are trying to do so.[14]

Manipur has been the home of several ethnic groups over the centuries. Almost nine-tenths of the area of Manipur is hilly regions and about seven hundred square miles comprise the fertile central valley. From ancient time, the central valley of Manipur has been the home of the Meetei while the surrounding hilly regions of the state are inhabited by the hill people (today they are known as the Nagas and the Kukis). All of them are known as Manipuris (including Meetei and Meetei Pangal) because they inhabit in Manipur. But Nagas and Kukis always claim that Meiteis are only Manipuris in order to assert their hidden agenda and also in the interest of balkanisation of Manipur.

Now-a-days hill folks are settled in different heartland areas of valley, living with love and affection by extending helping hands with Meiteis. There is no clash between them because they clearly understand their originality. Meiteis remain silent when Jadonang, a Naga leader killed four unarmed Manipuris, probably as sacrifice to his new god in 1929. As a result he was hanged on the 29August 1931.[15]It is undisputed fact that in the history of Manipur, hill people both Naga and Kuki accepted the valley king as the lord of the valley and the hills as well. His 'writ' ran not only in the hills now forming part of Manipur but even beyond it towards the north of Nagaland. The whole area looked upon the king as the supreme of all (sovereign).

In relationship between hill and valley people, they had different political and economic system on account of geographical condition and existing of some evil social practices. There were no mass-mixing among the different ethnic groups of highlanders and valley people due to having unsound communication system. Only the chiefs of highlanders could contact Meetei King and his valley subjects. Moreover there was not any good trade system. They were practising head hunting among the different tribes of highlanders in olden days simply in the womb of parochial political culture.

They feared each other from village to village and it was the result of their isolation and geographical barriers. In the earlier period of Manipur history, there was no hill leader who tried to give good messages to the masses for tribal unification. Instead of it, they were taking internecine action against each other and these evil reactions remain in the minds of different tribal groups. But in valley, the seven clans were united under the Meetei King and had common political aspiration, culture, religion and customs. In other words they were united under one name i.e. the Meetei, which was the tireless effort of the king. Most of the tribal chiefs were under his control. Most of the subjects of early period of hill and valley conceived the idea of Manipur as it was for both—hill and valley people. In 'Pena' (indigenous musical instrument) 'Eshei' (song), all the singers always started with blessings from God to hill and valley people. But main shortcoming of the Meetei king was that he did not make adequate provisions for the administration of the hills. Chiefs of the highlanders were also not giving any message about the close relationship with valley people. Moreover king and his nobler (including chiefs of highlanders) could not launch mass ethnic canvass of hill men as Meetei. It was confined only in the valley area so the factor of cleavage between the hill folks and valley people emerged. This was done due to existing local administration in the hill and monarchical form of government in the valley.

In reality, the king was the head of all the inhabitants of Manipur—both hill and valley. The kings of Manipur who ruled in the later part of history were not having the tendency and spirit of improving their administration towards the development of social, political and economic life for the both valley and hill people. They simply collected taxes from subjects in order to meet the British demands. There were forced labour commonly known as 'Chakthak' (feeding state servants), 'Yarek Shantri' (guarding the state servant at night when they came to villages), 'Chandon Senkhai' (subscription of a little amount of money for decorating *chandon*, a paste of sandal wood, on the forehead of all Hindu Meeteis), 'Pothang' (carrying luggage of state's nobility without payment) etc. Even they charged the tax of 'Mangba' (pollution or impure) and while he or she turned as 'Sengba' (clean or pure) by offering some money. The people of valley got the severed test of feudal system when the hill people simply had given tax to the British. Meiteis were really in grave condition when they were under the control of British and the native king. In short valley people were under the control of feudal lord and British colonial system. Before merging to the Indian Union the hill and valley of Manipur seem to exist separately having separate political culture and political socialisation with different methods. It was the seed sowed for germinating the theory of two sons of soil which is articulated in the minds of the hill and valley people.

After independence of Manipur on 14th August 1947, maximum effort was made by the ruling elites under the Manipur Constitution Act 1947 to bridge the gap between the two entities. But it lasted for a few months because Manipur was annexed to India in 1949. She was ruled by India just like the British with the political status of part 'C' state. There was no assembly and all the administrative functions were performed by the outsiders. All the facilities were confined to the valley areas only as a path of development. Thus the tendency of Naga integration or expansion of Nagaland and demanding of Kuki homeland has been increasing day by day within the territory of Manipur.

In a democratic set-up, politics may be operated in existing categories of people and institution. And in this process, categories of people change and so do the institutions. In a plural society like Manipur these groups have come to serve as the bases for political mobilisation. In an attempt to gain support, elites mainly political elites seek to manipulate the identity of the groups, therefore identity of the groups tends to be consolidated. But politics is also about acquiring power and getting a share of the resources which are always scarce. This makes the elites compete with one another in pushing the primary objectives of the group they represent. It is within this context where ethnicity manifests in its intensive forms resulting occasionally into the bursting of conflicts in violent forms.

The consolidated identity by the politics of 'devil's advocates' in the hills became eye opener to the underground leaders as well as civil society leaders. They could use all the devices of the democratic institutions and tried to invent a new history which is devoid of facts and full of concoction. These were further animated by the theory of deprivation as our existing democratic institution gave more and more space to them. For instance, the division of Manipuris population into scheduled tribes and other categories helps reinforced the 'tribal identity' (within internal differentiation) among the tribes which is further aggravated by their settlement in the remote areas. Separate reserved political seats also sharpen the sense of differences. It has contributed to a sense of belonging to common political and economic category and that feeling in turn is exploited by the elites.

Therefore it is the fusion of various forces—the attempts by the elites to construct a unified identity, nature of the state, policies of the state and resource competition—that together help to consolidate a Naga identity (with competition and conflicts within that fold) which seeks political unification on the basis of a shared ethnic identity with a territorial base. Both ethnicity and nationality are the expressions of a mere general process of identity formation. In the case of Naga through a process of assimilation and appropriation of symbols and cultural traits, though without a common language, the identity formation was slowly extended to envelop many different groups. Its (Naga) identity expands; their territorial claim also proportionately expands. These should be in vain as long as the majority of Manipuris work on common interest and the ruling elites play democratic politics. Instead, having different laws in one state and playing communal politics by the majority elites, automatically the cleavage will be larger day by day.

Notes and References

1. *The Imphal Free Press*, 26 January 2005, Imphal, p. 2.
2. Chakrabaty, Sanat K.; '*Wanted: An Ethnic Vision for North East*,' in Grassroots Options, vol. IV, Issue 3, Winter-Spring, Shillong, 2002/03, p. 12.
3. Hanum, Hurst; '*Autonomy, Sovereignty and Self-Determination*,' Washington DC, Salvama Press, 1989, pp. 28-37.
4. *Ibid.*
5. *Ibid.*
6. A report of NE regional seminar on '*Accords, Peace Process and Prospects of Civil Society and Peace Initiatives*,' organised by NEPI, Guwahati, September 7, 2007, p. 15.
7. Dhanabir Laishram, '*North East in Benthic Zone*,' Akansha Publishing House, New Delhi, p. 153.
8. *Ibid.*
9. V Sumi and K Timothy, '*Cry for Justice*,' (MIP, GPRN) date & place of publications not cited. pp. 36-60.
10. *Op.cit.* A report of NE regional seminar on '*Accords, Peace Process and Prospects of Civil Society and Peace Initiatives*.'

11. Bharat Bhusan, seminar paper on '*Ongoing Peace Process and Negotiations in NE India—An Analysis*,' organised by NEPI at Guwahati on 7-9 September 2005.
12. '*Pages of People Voice*,' vol. 4, number 2, April-June 2004, Palace compound, Imphal, published by ROE Units & CSD.
13. From the statement given by camp director Ito Tongbram of COFPAI (Committee For Peace and Integrity) campaign in 1995.
14. Seminar paper on '*Land Reforms and Ethnic Crisis in North East India*,' held on 27th and 28th July 2005 organised by MAKAIAS & History Department, M.U.
15. Reid, Robert; '*History of the frontier areas bordering on Assam*,' Eastern publishing House, Delhi, 1983, p. 86.

VI
Conclusion

Our nation is a federation made up of many federating units and princely states likewise to some extent of the formation of Australia, Canada, United States, USSR etc. Though, USSR was disintegrated in early 90s as it had the provision of right to secede from the union in its constitution. In the United Sates also there were turbulences to secede from the federation but all become worthless and also because of the provisions in the American constitution that excluding some lists like defence, currency etc. all are in the power of the federating units.

However the nature of Indian federation is different from all others as our founding fathers had borrowed provisions from the constitutions of different nations so as to suit the working of it. As a consequence there arise many discontentments for sharing the power between the Centre and the States.

To remove these, Sarkaria Commission was appointed in 1983 to look after the working of the Centre-State relations. The Commission gave its recommendations that need a strong Centre whereas States should also give their due share for better administration and economic activities. Still many provisions of those recommendations have not been expedited. Therefore, we are in mystery on how far our Centre-State relations are working and in which direction these have lead to. And thereby it leads to the emergence of various movements in different part of the country with special reference to north-east.

Regarding this, if we have to discuss the implications of identity crisis in Manipur, it is necessary to study the political aspiration of the Meitei, the majority community, who are at centre of the scale in the ethnic enmity between the Naga and Kuki. The Meitei are the only community in the world who can't settle in their own motherland and the people who have been denied the political right of candidature in their soil. In Manipur, there are some laws which are implemented in hill and valley separately. In other words, some laws are not common in hill and valley, like Manipur Panchayati Raj Act (MPRA), as it is not implemented in the hill areas.

Besides, because of tribal reserved constituency known as outer parliamentary constituency, more than

4 lakhs competent Meitei may cast their votes but without having any right of contesting election seeking the holding of office of Member of Parliament (MP). Still they are not included in the inner parliamentary constituency of valley (for MPs election only). Further if we look to the territory of Manipur, it was so large if one study from the report given by the British.[1] Moreover a good numbers of Meitei were in neighboring states and foreign countries mainly in Myanmar and Bangladesh. But Manipuri Diaspora was not at stake to be reorganised the state again; instead they are giving loyalty to their states though they are facing the problem of Bishnupriya issue in Assam and Bangladesh. They are extending their helping hands and contribute constructive views and ideas to protect territorial integrity of their motherland Manipur.

Again from her glorious past, it came to know that Manipuri people lived in a peaceful, jovial and prosperous life with a confer sense of pride on each one of them. Most of the people live together in an atmosphere of love, care and mutual sharing of responsibilities. However, the inedibility of this glorious past seems to be threatened to extinction by the animosities among the hill and the plain people of the present days. The existing condition of hill and that of plain people spelt out continuous conflicts, misunderstandings and miseries not only among the people of the respective tribes and groups but also to the governments of both the state and the Centre. There arise a big question that how it is happening in the hidden paradise on earth i.e. in Manipur. The genesis of it is external forces as they are coming of exogenous religion, British colonial rule and existing political economic system.

As consequence, the formation of ethnicity, emergence of ethnic nationalism and its ethnic armies are coming up in the state. The formation of ethnicity in North-east India presents a unique picture from their counterpart of the rest of India. This is also due to the fact of geo-political situation, historical background and influence of heterogeneous tribal group into the region. Manipur being a multi-ethnic society, ethnicity becomes an important instrument in demanding economic and political upliftment, which consequently leads to the consolidation of each ethnic group.

As by-product of above fact, another feature is compounded again in the political history of Manipur i.e. communal politics. The Meitei always defended when Nagas and Kukis raise the question of it. In its long history of post statehood politics, the post of Chief Ministership of Manipur was occupied for a maximum tenure by Yangmaso Saiza and Rishang Keising, both of whom hail from the community of so called Manipuri Naga. Even the minority Manipuri

Muslim leader Md. Alimuddin was the Chief Minister of Manipur when the people got statehood in 1972. Today tribal scholars claim that the majority Meitei legislators (40 out of total seats) always suppressed the voice of the minority i.e. Naga and Kukis since they are in majority in the state Assembly. Jonathan, a Naga member of Manipur Legislative Assembly commented, 'everything is concentrated only in Imphal Valley ... even the centrally sponsored schemes for the hill are always diverted to Imphal valley ... and false utilisation certificates were issued to the central government of India.'[2]

After all, in a democratic set-up, majority's will and voice always prevail and the minority's will and voice are always bound to be defeated. In this context, both the Nagas and Kukis wanted to increase their political seats in the state Legislative Assembly. It might be related with sudden changes of total population of hill areas in the 2001 and 2011 census report. It was really an unexpected increase of the number of population in the hill areas. As consequence, joint political parties of Manipur have demanded to the Centre that Manipur should be excluded from the delimitation exercise which is to be carried on the basis of the decadal census of 2001. This is simply the tug of war between hill and valley elites to have more reserved seats and on the other hand the Meitei elites want to maintain status quo of it. In short, whatever happens and is bound to happen have communal politics at its backdrop.

The Southern Naga Union of Nagaland states (SNUNS) stated in Manipur Hill voice that, 'there are brilliant tribal members in the Assembly and in the Council of Minister too. Yet, they are helpless when the time of voting comes. If you have to fight through for the cause of the minority, you are a fool. You have either to surrender your cause or to resign from the seat, whether as an MLA or a Cabinet Minister, or even as a Chief Minister if the majority will not to your plea. This is the exact position of our hill members in the Assembly today …'[3]

Furthermore a Naga scholar stated that large numbers of people are affected either directly or indirectly by the government and politics, because the common people depend upon the government for their livelihood. He (Naga scholar) illustrated with an example that, 'to start a school or college, to form a co-operative society, and sometime even to get into a college or obtain admission into a government hospital, one needs government. Further, the employed people whether they are transferred to another locality or not, whether they can obtain a loan, and whether they got promoted, all depends on the decisions of government officers. Thus, to get one of these things done, members of the state legislative assembly are among the most sought after elected official since they are in direct contact with the government administration.' According to him the tribal communities feel that they are left behind the valley people in every developmental aspect, because their elected representatives are always in the minority both in the government and in the opposition. From these pre-occupied feelings of minority in the political life of Manipur, they started their demand for a separate tribal state.[4]

In case of communal politics, the Meitei ruling elites are getting apprehension about the alteration of boundary because maximum Naga MLAs are in favour of Southern Nagaland. So they are compelled to play communal politics. Today, they have tendency to hold Chief Ministership only by the Meitei in order to protect the state boundary. Otherwise, communal politics should not have rooted in the political soil of Manipur. It is worthwhile to mention what had happened in the Representative House of Manipur in 1948. According to the Manipur State Constitution Act of 1947, under Article 17, it was in the ratio of 30:18:3, between General, Hills and Mohamadans with an additional two seats to represent educational and commercial interests.[5] Only the changes could be seen in the post-merger period.

During the last decades, Manipur have experienced crucial transformation in various domains of its political existence. Many movements were launched to eliminate King's rights. The formation of state as a part of Indian Union, active participation of people for changing monarchy to people representative government have brought significant changes in the attitudes of the masses as political actors with participant political culture. But the government response of spoon-feeding like giving Part 'C' State, Union Territory and finally Statehood created accumulated discontentment to the masses. The best example was the granting of statehood to Nagaland in 1963 while Manipur was in 1972.

As consequence, Naga people of Manipur (Manipuri Naga) conceived the ideas to merge with Nagaland. The political status was demanded by the people of each state with struggle. Only different thing is Nagas were on the path of violence and Manipuris believed in non-violence as such type of transformation in political domain is not democratic at all. For Manipur as sovereign state became part 'C' means third class status, it did not have its own Assembly. After the completion of 3rd Five Year Plan, Manipur got statehood. So many people argued that there was no justice in social, political and economic sphere as mentioned in the Preamble of our Constitution.

When Manipur became a full-fledged state on 21st January 1972, the Assembly constituencies were delimited into 60 seats. Out of which 20 are reserved seats for the scheduled tribes and one seat for the scheduled castes and the rest are for general or unreserved. The state is represented in the Lok Sabha by two members and sends one member in the Rajya Sabha. The Assembly constituencies of the state are demarcated and distributed according to the population as is the case of rest of the country. There are 9 (nine) districts in the state—five in the hill and four in the valley. The five districts in the hill are Chandel, Churachandpur, Senapati, Tamenglong and Ukhrul. The four districts in the valley are Bishnupur, Imphal East, Imphal West and Thoubal.

If one analyses about the seat allocation based on territorial size, it is true to say that seat allocation is uneven because 40 seats are distributed to the four districts in the valley while the remaining 20 seat are distributed to the five hill districts. These five hill district constitutes 9/10 of the total area of the state mainly inhabited by the two group Nagas and Kuki-Chins. But no one could claim that it is uneven allocation of seats because seat allocation or distribution is done according to the population basis. It is not an exceptional case only in Manipur, but followed throughout the country. Interestingly, the Naga elites reacted on large scale as big issue in their political movement. So the Naga political organisations like (South Nagas Union of Nagaland state) elaborating the opposition of the tribal members in the state Assembly stated that, 'in the state assembly, the tribal members affiliation to different political parties and their attachment to different ethnic group led to contradiction of ideas among themselves, and they are found to be handicapped to raise the issue when a matter of urgent importance arises covering the tribal, because of their individual survival and political compulsion.'[6]

Thus communal politics in Manipur could be visualised in the eyes of the masses of both-hill and valley by blaming each other. Now-a-days the critical new dimension is the various ethnic movements spearheaded by respective ethnic outfits as it would only hinder the economic status and growth of the common people instead of bringing about harmony. Therefore, the collective and collaborative efforts of the government, academicians and civil society organisations are significantly required in order to promote harmony and spirit of common brotherhood amongst all the people of the state. The majority communities should also give political space of them in order to avoid minority political exclusion with understanding of their political interest.

The state versus ethnic groups in Manipur with the identity card is also because of not having common political culture, socialisation and aspiration. Various ethnic movements have been launched in order to pressurise their demands and maintain separate political and ethnic identity of their respective groups. In reality the failure of this socialisation process is only the result of British's 'divide and rule policy.' The British colonial administration un-hesitantly encouraged all the ethnic movements in Manipur. The same formula was applied by government in the later part of the political history of the state.

But Nagas and Kukis are not thinking over the impact of these, instead they are heading to the fight each other by bearing the nomenclature given by the British i.e. the Nagas and Kukis. At the same time the Meiteis are also in the game of different treatment to the hill people mainly by political executive and temporary executive. Ultimately it has adversely affected the socio-political inspirational level in the valley and hill, basically after the post-merger period. Gradually, in the process of changes compounded with modernisation, the tribal elites play communal-card amongst the masses of hill for having their dreams of separate social and political identity. On this line, they politicise their people and have launched many movement which eventually lead to the threats of the state's territorial integrity.

From the very beginning, government is trying to solve this problem by granting autonomy to these so called marginalised groups. Under the Manipur Hill Areas Autonomous District Council Act, six autonomous district councils were constituted in order to enjoy some degree of autonomy. Since its election was held after a long gap, the present situation to the extent of delegating the powers is in puzzle. It is noted that development of all ethnic groups and minorities is possible if larger interests of the state are served. The demand for greater autonomy may come up more and more and also needs to accommodate it, although further division of existing state into a smaller and smaller one along the ethnic lines will not be a lasting solution. It also leads to micro level of exclusive politics verses inclusive politics in between hill-valley relationship. The Manipuri Meitei are claiming periphery to the Indian Union. In the same vein, the Manipuri Nagas and Manipuri Kukis claim themselves as periphery within periphery. Therefore it would be better to serve their aspiration by granting effective say in the management of their affairs particularly by creating an atmosphere of participant political culture where it will come only when the people come forward to recognise the incentives of it. Otherwise there would be echoes of claiming periphery within periphery again and again.

Notes and References

1. See TC Hodson, '*The Meithei's*,' DK Fine Art Press, Delhi, 1989, p. 1.
2. *Nagaland Page*, August 19, 2001.
3. South Naga Union of Nagaland State (SNUNS), *Manipur Hill Voices*, (Nagaland, SNUNS), 1992, pp. 12-13.
4. Memorandum submitted to Prime Minister of India on 18th July, 1980 by ATSUM.
5. '*The Manipur State Constitution Act. 1947*,' in Sanajaoba N (eds.); *Manipur Treaties and Documents (1110-1971)*, Vol. 1, New Delhi, Mittal Publications, 1993, p. 363.
6. Hitson, P.T. Jusho; '*Politics of Ethnicity in North East India*,' Regency Publications, New Delhi, 2004, p. 23.

Appendix-I

Manipur state constitution act, 1947

Whereas it is expedient to enact a law for the governance of the Manipur state, His Highness the Maharaja of Manipur is pleased to enact as follows:

Chapter I

1. Title: This Act shall be called the Manipur State Constitution Act 1947.

2. Extent and Application: This Act shall extend to the whole of the Manipur State inclusive of the Hill Areas saying that it shall not apply in any matter where a specific reservation of powers is made to any authority in the Hills under the provisions of the Manipur State Hill people's (Administration) Regulation, 1947.

3. Government of the State by His Highness the Maharajah: The territories for the time being and hereafter vested in the Maharajah are governed by and in the name of the Maharajah. All rights, authority and jurisdiction which appertain or are incidental to the Government of such territories are exercisable by the Maharajah subject to the provision of this Act.

4. Succession: Succession to the throne shall be governed by the Law of Primogeniture provided that the heir must be the legitimate son of a marriage recognised by the Council of Ministers. In the event of failure of heirs in the direct male line, His Highness the Maharajah shall, after consultation with the Council of Ministers and the Assembly, designate his heir.

5. **Attainment of Majority:** The Maharajah or his heir shall be taken to attain majority at the age of 21 years.

6. **Council of Regency:** (a) Where by reason of the Maharajah being a minor or where by reason of any mental defect or grave bodily sickness as a result of which the Maharajah becomes permanently incapable of exercising his powers, the Council of Ministers shall take steps to set up a Council of Regency which shall exercise those powers in the State and shall continue in office for such time as the Council may determine;

(b) Notwithstanding the provisions of Sub-Section (a) above, the Maharajah in consultation with Council of Ministers may at any time or for any reason which may appear suitable, set up a Council of Regency to exercise his functions;

(c) A Council of Regency set up under Sub-Section (a) and (b) above, may comprise of one or more persons as may seem desirable, the Regent or Council of Regency shall before taking office be required to take an Oath before the State Assembly to be loyal to the state and to observe faithfully its Constitution and Laws;

(d) Where in any event it shall be necessary to set up a Council of Regency either for the reasons laid down in sub-sections (a) and (b) above or for any other reason or where for any reason the Maharajah has become incapable of exercising his powers before such regency can be set up, the Council of Ministers shall take whatever steps may be necessary for the governance of the State till such time as the Regency is created.

7. Failure of Heirs and Disputed Succession: (a) In the event of failure of heirs in the direct male line and the failure of the Maharajah to designate his Heir under section 4 above, a joint extraordinary session of the State Assembly and the Council of Ministers shall immediately be convened and shall remain in closed and continuous session till it shall have determined by a 75% majority of the members present and voting, the person to whom the throne shall pass;

(b) Where for any reason the succession to the throne is disputed, the Council of Ministers shall, on the death of the Ruler, take such steps as may immediately be necessary for the good governance of the State and shall refer the matter under dispute to the Chief Court for decision. Where any party is aggrieved by the decision of the Chief Court, an appeal shall lay to such authority as may be determined hereafter.

8. The Maharajah's Prerogatives: (a) All family

matters which are the Maharajah's sole concern as head of the ruling family, all matters which are his sole concern as the defender of faith and all matters connected with titles, Honours and Palace ceremonial shall be deemed to fall within the Maharajah's personal prerogative and in such matters the Maharajah shall exercise full discretion subject to the provisions of the Constitution and the law of the State.

The Maharajah's prerogative shall not; however, be taken to comprise any matter wherein the legitimate interests of the State administration or a civil right sustainable in a court of law is involved. It will be within the prerogative of the Maharajah to remit punishment and pardon offenders subject to the provisions of the Manipur State Court's Act provided that this prerogative shall not prejudice the right of any individual to compensation;

(b) It shall be the prerogative of the Maharajah and the Maharani that neither may be made answerable at law or subject to any legal proceeding in the state courts. Their persons and property shall be inviolable;

(c) Notwithstanding section 8(b) above, it shall be lawful for the state council in consultation with the chief court to draw up a statement of charges against the Maharajah or the Maharani where it is proved beyond all possible doubt that the Maharajah or the Maharani has been guilty of murder or any other heinous offence or of any extreme political crime against the provisions of the constitution;

(d) On a statement of charges being drawn up under clause (c) above, the council shall present it before the Maharajah or the Maharani and require satisfaction. Should satisfaction be not forthcoming the council may refer the matter to such authority as may be determine hereafter.

II
Definitions

9. In this Act and the Rules issued thereunder unless there is something repugnant to the subject or the context:

(a) State shall mean the Manipur state comprising the whole territory of Manipur as delineated in the maps of the survey of India current at the date of this enactment;
(b) The Maharajah means his highness the Maharajah of Manipur, the constitutional head of the state;
(c) Chief Minister means the officer entrusted with the chief executive functions of the state;
(d) Minister means a member of the Council of Ministers appointed under this Act by name or by virtue of his office to administer certain branches of the state administration and to

perform the duties and exercise the power imposed and conferred upon a minister by this Act and Rules framed thereunder;

(e) Council means the state council of ministers constituted under this Act;

(f) Assembly means the state assembly as constituted under this Act;

(g) Gazette means the official journal of the state by means of which important orders, notices, communiqués, etc., are published;

(h) Speaker means the president of the Assembly and includes the deputy speaker in the absence of the speaker or in the absence of both a member voted to the chair;

(i) Civil list means the appropriation of funds for the expenses of the ruling family and the privy purse of the ruler;

(j) Privy Purse means such portion of the Civil List as is appropriated exclusively for the personal expenses of the Maharajah;

(k) Revenue includes all receipts of the state from state assets, from all lands, forests, taxes, fines, penalties, forfeitures, lapse and other sources;

(l) Rules means any rule issued under this Act;

(m) Fundamental rights shall mean those rights which the state people shall enjoy as of right under this act;

(n) The pronoun 'he' and its derivatives are used of any person whether male or female.

Chapter III
The Executive

10. Council of Ministers: (a) subject to the provisions of this Act and subject also to the provisions of the Rules for the administration of the Manipur state, the executive authority of the state is delegated to and shall vest in the council of ministers;

(b) Where under this Act or the rules for the administration of the state, it is requisite that the approval of the Maharajah shall be taken to any measure, the Chief Minister shall seek the approval of the Maharajah in person or in writing and shall obtain the Maharajah's orders thereon. Should in any case the Maharajah's approval be withheld, the Maharajah shall be pleased to inform the reasons for withholding such approval in writing to the council;

(c) The Council of Ministers shall consist of the Chief Minister and six other ministers;

(d) The six ministers on the council shall be elected by the state assembly subject to the provision that two of these ministers shall be representatives of the hill people of the state elected in such manner as shall be laid down in the rules of business of the state assembly;

(e) The Chief Minister shall be appointed by the Maharajah in consultation with the elected ministers on the council;

(f) The Chief Minister and Ministers shall receive letters of appointment over the seal of Maharajah;

(g) The Chief Minister in consultation with the Ministers shall allot portfolios.

11. The Chief Minister shall be the President of the Council and the Vice-President shall be appointed by the Council.

12. The Council of Ministers shall have a common seal and shall be jointly responsible to the Maharajah for the administration of the State.

13. The Council of Ministers and the Ministers individually shall exercise such powers and functions as may be assigned to them by or under this Act or under the Rules for the Administration of the State.

14. The quorum necessary for the transaction of business at a meeting of the Council shall not be less than three excluding the president.

15. The Chief Minister and Ministers shall, on taking office, swear an oath of loyalty and allegiance to the Maharajah in the following form:

> 'I (Name of Minister) have been appointed as a Member of the Manipur State Council do solemnly swear that I will be loyal and faithful and bear true allegiance to the Maharajah his heirs and successors and that I will faithfully discharge the duties laid on me under this Act.'

16. A Minister of the Council shall not be removable from office except in accordance with the provisions of Chapter IV below.

Chapter IV
The State Assembly

17. There shall be constituted a State Assembly. The Assembly shall be elected for a period of three years and shall comprise representatives freely elected by the people on an adult franchise and on the principle of Joint Electorate. Elections shall be in such manner and by such franchise as may be laid down under the Rules for the elections to the State Assembly provided always that the Representatives returnable from General, Hill and Mohamadans Constituencies shall be in the ratios of 30: 18: 3 respectively with an additional two seats for the Representatives of Educational and commercial interests.

18. The State Assembly may debate all matters concerning the Government and well-being of the State which, in the opinion of five Members of the Assembly, it is in the public interest to debate. The Assembly shall tender such advice to the Council of Ministers in any matter in which a majority of the Members present, are agreed on the advice which shall be tendered provided that no matter touching the Maharajah's Prerogative shall be debated and provided

that the Maharajah may on the advice of the Council, veto debate on any matter where such course shall in the public interest be necessary.

19. The State Assembly shall not tender advice to the Council on any matter which is of primary concern to the Hill people unless such advice has the support of a majority of the Hill Representatives in the Assembly.

20. Subject to the provisions of this Act, the Assembly may make rules for regulating its proceedings and the conduct of Business;

21. Where in any case it is required to pass a vote of no confidence against a Minister of the Council for his individual acts, a motion of no confidence, signed by not less than ten members of the Assembly and laying out in detail, the facts giving rise to the motion, may with the permission of the Speaker of the Assembly be moved. If such motion shall receive the support of at least 75 per cent of the members present and voting, it shall be forwarded through the Chief Minister to the Maharajah, who, unless there appear strong and valid reasons to the contrary which shall be recorded in writing, shall after consultation with the Chief Minister require the Minister against whom the motion has been passed to resign;

22. Where in any case the State Council or the Maharajah is in the special circumstances of any case

unable to accept the advice of the Assembly, the Maharajah or the Council as the case may be, shall communicate in writing the reasons which have led to such course and shall give facilities for personal discussion of the matter with a representative or representatives deputed by the Assembly;

23. Subject to the provisions of this Act and the Rules framed under it for the disposal of the Assembly business, there shall be Freedom of Speech in the Assembly and no member shall be liable to any proceedings in any court in respect of any speech or vote given by him in the Assembly or a committee thereof and no person shall be liable in respect of any publication by or under the authority of the Assembly of any report, paper, vote or proceedings;

24. No member of the Assembly shall be liable to arrest or detention in prison under a Civil process:

(a) If he is a member of the Assembly, during the continuance of the Assembly.

(b) If he is a member of any committee of the Assembly, during the continuance of the meeting of the Committee.

25. The elected Ministers, the Speaker, Deputy Speaker and members of the Assembly shall receive such emoluments as may be determined from time to time by the Assembly.

Chapter V
The Law Making Authority

26. The Law Making Authority in the State shall consist of the Maharajah in Council in collaboration with the State Assembly acting under Section 18, above.

27. When the Council or the Assembly consider that a law should be enacted the Council shall cause a Bill to be drafted, which shall be laid before the Assembly and a reasonable time shall be given for consideration thereof. The Council shall then cause to be made such alterations or amendments as may be deemed necessary in the light of the advice tendered by the Assembly and the Chief Minister shall submit the Bill in its final form for the assent of the Maharajah.

28. On the receipt of the Maharajah's assent the Bill shall be published in the State Gazette and shall become an Act having the force of law.

29. Should the Maharajah in any case withhold his Assent to a Bill, the Bill shall lapse as if it had not been passed. If the assent of the Maharajah is not forthcoming within one calendar month of the bill being submitted to him, he shall be deemed to have withheld his assent.

30. Where the Assent of the Maharajah to any Bill is withheld, the Council may cause the same Bill to be

introduced in the next session of the Assembly and if passed without amendment by a 75 per cent majority of the Assembly, the Bill shall be certified over the Seal of the Council and shall become law.

31. Nothing in this Chapter shall be deemed to derogate from the absolute right of the Maharajah in Council to promulgate, in emergency cases, orders having the force of the law without previous reference to the Assembly where the public interest in their opinion demands that such order shall be promulgated provided that the first opportunity shall be taken of laying the order before the Assembly for consideration. Any such order shall not have the force of law for a period of more than six months.

Chapter VI
Finance

32. The Revenue of the State and such other receipts as may accure from whatever source, less such reasonable percentage of the total real revenue as may be reserved for the Civil List, are placed at the disposal of the Council for expenditure on the Government of the State in the manner prescribed by the State Account Rules saving that in every year a sum representing not less than 17 per cent of the average real revenue of the State for the preceding three years shall be allocated for expenditure on the welfare and administration of the Hill people.

33. The Minister in charge of Finance shall prepare an annual budget showing the estimated receipts and expenditure for the ensuing year classified under the prescribed heads of account and shall submit it to the Assembly within fifteen days of its meeting for the budget session along with a statement of account for the previous year.

34. The Assembly shall after considering the budget, submit it with their recommendation to the Council, who, having made such modifications as may be deemed necessary shall submit it to the Maharajah for approval. Where any delay occurs in the granting of assent to the budget by the Maharajah and where such assent has not been obtained by the first day of the financial year, provisional effect shall be given to the budget as passed by the Assembly and funds shall be drawn against its provisions as it had received assent.

35. The Maharajah's Civil List shall be fixed at a figure equal to 10 per cent of the real revenues of the State over the preceding three years, provided that no extraordinary revenues shall be taken into account when determining this amount and provided that no State revenue in excess of Rupees twenty lakhs shall be taken into account in any one year. The appropriations to the Maharajah's Civil List shall be non-votable and shall not be the subject of debate in the Assembly.

36. No tax whatsoever shall be shown in the budget and no tax shall be collected by any officer of the State or by any person unless such tax has been imposed by due process of Law.

37 (a) There shall be a State Auditor who shall be appointed by the Maharajah in Council on a nomination to be made by the Comptroller of Audit, Assam or such other officer as may be deemed suitable. Such nominee shall be employed on contract for a period of not less than five years and shall be removed only by the Maharajah in Council in consultation with the authority making the nomination;

(b) The conditions of Service of the State Auditor shall be such as may be prescribed by the Maharajah in Council provided always that he shall not be eligible for any office of profit in the State after his retirement.

(c) The Auditor shall exercise such powers and perform such duties as may be laid down in the State Account Rules.

Chapter VII
Hill People

38. The Council shall be responsible for the welfare and the good administration of the Hill people of the State and shall provide such funds for this purpose as may, subject to the provision of Section 32 above, be

deemed necessary, provided that the local authorities in the Hill shall exercise such powers of local self-government as may be laid down in the Manipur State Hill (Administration) Regulation, 1947.

Chapter VIII
The Services

39. The Council shall issue rules regulating the conditions of Service in the departments of the State.

40. A Manipur State Appointments Board shall be constituted and the Council shall issue rule regulating the constitution, functions and procedure of the Board. The Board shall consist of not less than three members, one of whom must be a Hillman and a chairman and shall be the final authority in all matters connected with appointments and promotions to the State service except in so far as specific powers may be reserved under this Act or the Rules for Administration of the State.

Chapter IX
The Judicature

41 (a) There shall be a complete separation of the Judiciary from the Executive;

(b) The Judicature of the State shall be as laid down in the Manipur State Courts Act, 1947.

42. The Chief Justice of the State and two Puisne Judges shall be appointed by the Maharajah in Council under the Royal Seal and shall hold office until the age of 65 years provided that:

(a) A Judge may resign his office;

(b) A Judge may be removed from his office by the Maharajah in Council only on the grounds of misbehaviour or of infirmity of body or mind.

43. A person shall not be appointed as a Judge of the Chief Court unless he:

(a) be a graduate in law and has held Judicial Office at least for Five years;

(b) is a barrister qualified in England of five years' standing, or

(c) has for at least five years held judicial office in British India in a post not inferior to that of a subordinate judge; or

(d) has for at least a period of ten years been a pleader of any High Court or of the Manipur Chief Court; or

(e) be a person recognised as having a special capacity for the exercise of Judicial functions.

Chapter X
Fundamental Rights and Duties of Citizenship

44. All citizens shall be equal before the law. Titles and other privileges of birth shall not be recognised in the eyes of law.

45. The liberty of the individual shall be guaranteed. No person may be subjected to any judicial interrogation or placed under arrest or be in any other way deprived of his liberty save as provided by law.

46. No person shall be tried save by a competent Court.

47. No person may be tried except by a competent Court who shall give full opportunity to such person to defend himself by all legal means.

48. All penalties shall be as determined by law.

49. Capital punishment may not be inflicted for purely political crimes.

50. No citizen may be banished from the State, expelled from one part of the country to another, and obliged to reside in a specific place save in such cases as may be expressly determined by law.

51. Every dwelling shall be inviolable save under express provision of law.

52. There shall be guaranteed to all people, justice, social, economic and political; equality of status, of opportunity and before the law; freedom of thought, expression of belief, faith, worship, vocation, association, and action, subject to law and public morality.

53. The practice of Arts and Sciences shall be unrestricted and shall enjoy the protection and support of the State.

54. Without any prejudice to the communities concerned, public institutions shall be opened to all the citizens of the State.

55. (a) All officials of the State or of a local Government shall be answerable before the law for their individual and unlawful actions.

(b) Where damage is caused to an individual by the act of an official of the State or an official of a Local Government, such individual may sue the State before the Chief Court and may seek redress save where such damage has been caused by a bonafide act of a State servant in pursuance of a policy duly laid down by a competent authority.

Chapter XI
General Clauses

56. Any provision of this act may be subject to amendment by the Maharajah in Council provided

that such amendment is laid before the Assembly and receives the support of at least 80 per cent of the members of the State Assembly present and voting, when such amendment is debated.

57. Where in any case circumstances arise which prevent the proper operation in law or spirit of this Constitution Act, the Council may at their discretion refer the matter for decision to such authority outside the State as may be decided hereafter and the decision of that authority shall be binding.

58. The Court language of the State shall be Manipuri or English.

Bodh Chandra Singh
Maharajah of Manipur

Appendix-II

Inauguration of the First Manipur State Assemblly on October 18, 1948

Proclamation of his Highness Maharajah Bodhchandra

Members of the Manipur State Assembly Present

Introduction

This is the first time I as a Representative of Manipur Crown and Monarchy, unbroken and safeguarded with the blood of my forefathers for about two thousand years, address the First Assembly of the Manipur State on this historic day following the modern practice and British style. I consider myself fortunate to see the birth of an Assembly in the State during my time and again I feel proud to be able to place on record and make it known to the rest of India that though painted otherwise abroad, my state for the first time in India has, *just* as the Sun rises earlier in the east, taken the lead in the direction of democratic government, based on adult franchise and joint electorate in the line of which India is soon following. I take more pride in that though in countries like England; responsible government has been the outcome of the blood of so many persons, there has been in my state no bloodshed since I took the initiative here.

The New Constitution

While I have been all along anxious to accord responsible government, I have been sincerely watching as to the practicability or impracticability of the Constitution Act I now bring to the mind of the people that I had transferred my powers and responsibilities other than those of a Constitutional Ruler to the State Council since 1st July 1947 before the lapse of the British paramountcy and since then, I have already remained as a Constitutional Ruler. But most of the people are innocent as they have been imputing to me the actions of the Council. My only earnest wish is to see a more prosperous Manipur. Though the literacy is below five per cent, you have had the best opportunities, as afforded by a responsible government to serve your country to the fullest extent you desire with toleration and concord to make Manipur a greater Manipur.

Aim

Administrators and citizens of the State, in order that the integrity and separate entity of the State is preserved for ever as heretofore ensured by Pandit Jawaharlal Nehru, I wish to attach the highest measure of importance to detailing some account of what the State Manipur is-I mean the State and people, whom you now represent and on whose better administration, you are now out to embark.

Historical Background

To begin with, I feel a sudden emotion in my heart-I mean the sweet reminiscences of the past history of Manipur. Let the patriots fight for today. I will see that yesterday shines once more before the people ignorant of the beauty of yesterday. I am sure; a look back to the history of our land will at once inspire your mind towards greater and nobler deeds to prove your worth as worthy sons of worthy fathers.

Look the sweet and green valley with the sweeter and greener hills all round along the easternmost part of India-a smiling land, hallowed by footprints of heroes and admired as the Switzerland of India by strangers. It is Manipur, a salubrious land of hoary antiquity-a land of gems. Geographically, it is singularly isolated from the rest of India. Strategically, nature impresses on her a stamp of unity by fully encircling her with lofty mountains and hills making it an impregnable fortress and bulwark of defence doing the sentinel for the millions in India. She was a star in the eastern political firmament of India. Strong nations of the world covet her natural position. Such is Manipur.

Read her political history from 24 A. D. She had her dominion over a wide area extending as far as the southern portion of China in the north, the gold mines in the Sibasagar valley, the river Chindwin in the east and south, and Chandra pore (Cachar) in the west. Her present area is 8,650 square miles plus 7,000 square miles of the Kabaw valley, including 7,900 square miles of the hills. Read the war operations of Maharajah Garibniwaza in 1711, which shows how far the spirit of heroism and independence ran rampant in the veins of our forefathers. Read the Treaty of Maharajah Gourashyam and Mr. Verelst of the East India Company at Chittagong on the 14th September 1762, which shows the vast wealth and economic status of Manipur. Read the Treaty of Yandaboo, dated the 9th January 1834 ratified between Maharajah Gambhir Singh and the Company. This Treaty left for us a good heritage, namely the Kabaw valley of 7,000 square miles for which we now get from Burma Rs. 6,270 as annual tribute which according to the spirit of the terms of the Agreement, will cease when the area is riverted to our State. Maharaja Gambhir Singh died of disappointment for this loss of territory under duress. Sreejut Nara Singh's role in redeeming Manipur from Burma, when she was devastated and dismembered for 7 years was very great. Manipur was thus, by reason of her vast territories and economic resources, self-supporting as a self-contained unit. Her sphere of influence and mercantile activities was very wide. During the British rule, foreign goods gave a dulling effect to the indigenous products by dumping operations. Now is the best time to revive all these vanquished industries. Attempts are now being made to recover the losses of territories as in Cachar under duress.

Unity of Hill and Valley

All these times when Manipur was in the height of her power, 'Hill and Valley' were one; and this oneness defended Manipur against all invasions and thus, she could maintain her independence upto 1891, when the rest of India had already been conquered by the British. British conquest of this land resulted from the slackened unity between the Valley and Hills. Now, since the withdrawal of British paramountcy after 56 years' rule, we have reinforced the union of Hill and Valley; and best opportunities have reached us in order to work hand-in-hand towards achieving the common object of progress and national prosperity. The relation has become one of complete understanding and active sympathy; and it must be so, for Manipur is one and the hopes and aspirations of Hill and Valley are identical.

Manipur's Position in the Dominion of India

These are great days; great destinies are gathering momentum; great ideas are occupying the hearts of men and great causes have aroused great enthusiasms and great sacrifices. Amid the interplay of world forces India comes out stronger than before and Manipur too as a component part is the same with the removal of artificial hedge between Hill and Valley. I believe the sons of Manipur will be alive to it. In the large galaxy of heroes in the imperishable roll of honour, there were and there are now and there will never cease to be, beloved Manipuri names testifying to the fact that our people would rather die unsullied than outlive the disgrace of surrender to any measure that work prejudicial to the preservation of the separate entity of the State, while fostering the good and cordial relations with the Dominion of India. I am confident that the members of the Assembly will please see that this fair record is never breached.

State Finance Based in a Sound Economic Planning

A strong government means a government with a strong financial infrastructure. In order to ensure finance, a well thought out economic planning is necessary. I lay special stress on it, for a totally unplanned economy is a totally unplanned nation. I invite your attention to the inevitability of this economic planning so that you may be prepared to cope with it before the State finance assumes threatening proportions. The inexhaustible sources of her economic potentialities are already there, as it is provided by nature. What only wants is the *modus operandi* for increased productivity. The people will have to cultivate thriftiness, since the present rate of the flowing out of people's money in exchange of less important articles will jeopardize, at no distant date, the economic status of the individuals constituting the nation.

If the entire area of the State is properly explored and the sources are tapped, there is every possibility of the State's having one crore of rupees as annual income enabling us at the same time to produce all our requirements. Places like Jiribam and Moreh, if properly industrialised with the running of saw-mills, cotton mills, paper mills, etc., will bring huge incomes to the State. Manipur has been declared the best place for installing hydro-electric plants. There are points which can feed the entire Assam with hydro-electric power on commercial basis too. There should be industrial Centers at strategic places-Hill and Valley-equipped with modern techniques and modern technology. I shall be glad to see Hill towns properly electrified, springing up. I desire that prior consideration be given to the construction of roads in the hills in order to facilitate communications. There are now only one lakh of *paris* of land thrown open to cultivation. There is ten times the space still available for agricultural operations. Plantation of betelnut, tea and jute also may be introduced successfully in the now neglected but fertile soils. Export should outpace the import. During my long tours in the hills, I was deeply impressed with the yet surviving cottage industries which can stand any competition. The consequences of the war heavily told upon the raw materials. Charkha and handlooms have been the essential marriage gifts to our mothers and sisters. In redressing economic problems these should be developed. As regards the raw materials, eastern

Kasom still stands a living testimony. *Khaddar* is not a new thing here but rather-I should say-it originated from Manipur. The silk industry from cocoons is a long standing industry here. The Muga of Khurkhul remains unrivalled and unapproached in India. Rural reconstruction schemes be implemented in order to achieve all-round progress.

Education

Prior consideration should ago be given to education. I wish to see at least a High School in each of the Tehsils and important centres in the hills with good communications. While pursuing our future educational policy, we should be prepared to select more practical courses to suit the mode of our national life. Indigenous science of medicine and treatment should also be promoted. Fine Arts also have received the appreciation of the world. It attracted the world-poet Rabindranath Tagore also. Sir Akbar Hydari, His Excellency, the Governor of Assam, also highly encouraged it.

Our Part in the Individual and Collective Responsibility for Frontier Protection and Defence of Manipur in Particular

Manipur should be made militarily strong as, in the contemporary world; militia is the noblest estate of mankind. In the history and accounts of 1874, written by Col. Johnstone, you will come across that Manipuri nation constituted the best armies in the world. In January 1947, I apprised India Government through the Chamber of Princes, of the need for a strong Eastern frontier protecting military installations in order to safeguard Manipur in particular and India as a whole, as a result of the withdrawal of British paramountcy from India and Burma. But India Government has not yet communicated their final plan in this matter.

Now as from today, you have joined responsible government. I feel it my duty to point out, in the interest of this country and Commonwealth that it should be our individual and collective responsibility to work out a scheme for frontier protection, in collaboration with the Central Government. The present situation calls for immediate action in this respect. Since we are sincere, I am confident that the Central Government will give us proper and timely assistance with subsidies and finance and equipment. In the meantime with what little finance, we have, we should raise. Our small force to an efficient standard as home-guard without further delay. The inherent warlike spirit of the Manipuris should be maintained for the noble cause of India. Peace here in Manipur will be a fine contribution to India Government, while they are moulding India's destiny to enable her to stand up as one of the most powerful nations in the world.

The paramount importance of the strategic location of Manipur for defence and security reasons of India deserves the careful attention of enlightened governments; and we should be mindful of the benefits that we may render to our Dominion from her position, if we seriously depend on it.

Time is now roughly going on in the world and as such, it is a critical phase of Manipur too. Nevertheless, it is the best time for you to serve your mother-country while she needs and to prove that you are her worthy sons. You are to show to the world and to your people, the achievements or progress of the welfare of the people under this new government with clear results of a change for the better. Otherwise, the name "Responsible Government" may not be worth the name and the next step will be for the Constitutional Ruler to judge.

Our Guiding Principles

We should not forget that we are Manipuris, destined to live in Manipur and die in Manipur. Providence has bound our fates together indissolubly.

Leaders of the nation while undertaking to finance economic planning-long and short-for the material progress of the country in the nearest future, I want to make it a watchword that the means of increasing the State revenues from other sources are devised without causing hardship or burden to the people. I expect that every one of you, as a part of his obligation, will take care to acquaint himself with the mode of life on hills too by studying the four walls of the territory of Manipur, he is now going to govern. Send students abroad to foreign lands that they may bring back knowledge with which they may do service to her, but they should not bring ideas and ways of life that do not always conform to the environment of Manipur.

I wish to see you all becoming great and noble-noble, not for your own sake but noble for the country—to make Manipur great, a greater Manipur to enable her to stand up with head erect among the nations, as she did in the past. Work that Manipur may prosper. Suffer that Manipur may rejoice. Unite that Manipur may be strong.

Do the right that you may be brave. Whether you use pen or tongue, let your hearts be pure; and your resolve, mainly. The prosperity of a nation does not depend on the number of buildings, but it depends on the number of men of character—that is, radiant man of well-disciplined mould. I shall always remain aglow with the splendour of destiny of our people.

In finally, I call upon you all to take this as your motto and to join with me in a fervent prayer for the well-being of our Motherland.

Select Bibliography

i) Authored Books

Anthony D. Smith, '*Nationality and Identity*,' London: University of Nevada Press, 1993.

Alexander Mackenzie, '*The North East Frontier of British India*,' Mittal Publications, Delhi, 1981.

Captain Butler quoted by G.A. Grierson, '*Linguistic Survey of India*,' vol. 3. Part.2. Delhi, 1967.

Clifford Geertz, '*The Interpretation of Culture: Selected Essays*,' New York, Basic Books, 1973.

Constantine R., '*Manipur, Maid of the Mountains*,' New Delhi, Lancers publishers.

Dhanabir Laishram, '*North East in Benthic Zone*,' Akansha Publishing House, New Delhi, 2007.

——, '*Chaokhatpa Khunnai Amasung Meeyam*,' Imphal, 2000.

Erik H Erickson, '*Identity and the Life Cycle: Selected Papers*,' New York. International University Press, 1959.

——, '*Young Man Luther*,' New York: Norton. 1958.

Erik H Erickson, '*Identity: Youth and Crisis*,' 3 Queen Square, London, Faber and Faber: 1971.

Elly, E.B., '*Military Report on the Chin-Lushai Country*,' First published in 1893. FirmaKLM (P) Ltd. Calcutta, 1978.

Gangmumei Kamei, '*Ethnicity and Social Change: An Anthology of Essay*,' Imphal. 2002.

Gabriel A. Almond and G. Bingham Powell, Jr., '*Comparative Politics: A Developmental Approach*,' Amerind, New Delhi 1972.

Haobam Indrakumar, '*Basic Dimension of Identity and Integration; A Critical Appraisal on Meitei Perspective*,' Imphal, 2002.

Hurst Hanum, '*Autonomy, Sovereignty and Self-determination*,' Washington DC, Salvama Press, 1989.

H.V. Wiseman, '*Political System: Some Sociological Approaches*,' London: Routledge and Kegan Paul, 1966.

Jyotirmoy Roy, '*History of Manipur*,' Eastlight Publishing House, Calcutta, 1973.

W.S. Johnson Anal, '*The Pakan Tribes of Manipur*,' The Anal Naga Student's Union, Manipur, 1994.

Khelchandra N., '*Naothingkhong Phambal Kaba*,' Imphal, 1995.

L.M. Ibungohal, '*Introduction to Manipur*,' Imphal, 1963.

M. Chandra Singh, '*Panthoibi Khongul*', Imphal, 1999.

M. Alemchiba, '*A Historical Account of Nagaland*,' Naga Institute of Culture, Kohima.

M. Horam, '*Naga Polity*,' Low Price Publications, Delhi, 1992.

P.T. Hitson Jusho, '*Politics of Ethnicity in North East India*,' Regency Publications, New Delhi, 2004.

R.K. Jhaljit Singh, '*A Short History of Manipur*,' Imphal, 1965.

R.P. Singh, '*Electoral Politics in Manipur*,' Concept Publishing Company, New Delhi, 1981.

Roland Robertson (Ed.), '*Identity and Authority*,' Oxford: Basil Blackwell, 1980.

R.R. Shimray, '*Origin and Culture of Nagas*,' Somsok Publications, New Delhi, 1985.

R. Vashum, '*Nagas Right to Self-determination; An Anthropological-historical Perspective*,' Mittal publications, New Delhi, 2000.

T.C. Hodson, '*The Naga Tribes of Manipur*,' Neeraj Publishing House, Delhi, 1984.

TC Hodson, '*The Meithei's*,' DK Fine Art Press, Delhi, 1989.

Y.L. Roland Shimmi, '*Comparative History of Nagas; from Ancient Period till 1826*,' Inter India Publications, New Delhi, 1988.

ii) Edited

A Shimray, '*An Introduction to the Ethnic Problem in Manipur*,' New Delhi, undated

David Bloomfield and Ben Reilly (eds.), '*Democracy and Deep Rooted Conflict: Options for Negotiators*,' Stockholm: IDEA, 1998.

K.S. Aggarwal, (eds.), '*Dynamics of Identity and Inter-group Relations in NE India*,' Simla, Indian Institute of Advanced Study, 1999.

Lash, Scott and Jonathan Friedman (eds.), 'Modernity and Identity,' Oxford and Cambridge. Massachusetts. Blackwell, 1992.

Naorem Sanajaoba (eds.) 'Manipur Past and Present,' vol. 1, Mittal Publications, New Delhi, 1998.

——, 'Manipur Past and Present,' vol. 2.

——, 'Manipur Past And Present,' Vol. 3.

Nuh, V.K. (Compiled) and Lasuh, Wetshokhrolo (Ed)., 'The Naga Chronicle,' Regency Publications. New Delhi, 2002.

Pakem,B (eds.) 'Nationality, Ethnicity and Cultural Identity in North East India,' Omsons Publications, Guwahati, 1990.

iii) Dictionaries and Encyclopedia's;

David L Sills, '*International Encyclopedia of Social Sciences*,' vol. 3 and vol. 4. New York, McMillan Company and Free Press 1972.

Danbury, '*The Encyclopedia Americana*,' International edition, Grolier Incorporated, 1999.

John Ayto, Bloomsbury, '*Dictionary of Word Origin*,' 86, UB Delhi. Goyal Jawahar Nagar Saab, 1st Indian edition, 75 editions, 1990.

James Hastings, '*Encyclopedia of Religion and Ethics*,' vol. 8, Charls Scribners Sons, New York, 1964.

JA Simpson and E.S.C. Weiner (eds.), '*The Oxford English Dictionary*,' Oxford: Clarendon Press, 1989, second edition, vol. VII.

Encyclopaedia Incorporation, Chicago, '*The New Encyclopedia Britannica*,' vol. 13. 1962.

iv) Gazetteer's & Official Documents

EW Dun, '*Gazetteer of Manipur*,' Manas Publications, New Delhi, 1992.

Robert Reid, '*History of the Frontier Areas Bordering Assam; from 1883-1941*,' Eastern Publishing House, Delhi, 1983.

W. Mc Culloch, *An Account of the valley of Manipur*,' Calcutta. 1859.

Sanajaoba N. '*Manipur Treaties and Documents (1110-1971)*,' Vol. 1 & II, Mittal publications, New Delhi, 1993.

SK Sharma and Usha Sharma,: '*Documents on North East India*,' Vol. 6, Mittal Publication, 2006.

The Manipur State Constitution Act. 1947.

v) Journal

Journal of the American Psychoanalytic Association: 9, 1954.

Grassroots Options, vol. IV, issue 3, Winter-Spring, Shillong, 2002-03.

'*Crisis of identity in Manipur*,' *Journal of MU Research Club*, Imphal, 1997.

'*Pages of People Voice*,' vol. 4, number 2, April-June, 2004, Palace Compound, Imphal, published by ROE Units & CSD.

Sanathong, Monthly Journal, Imphal, June 2004, vol. 10. issue 4.

vi) Seminar Papers & Unpublished Articles

T. S. Gangte, 'Land problem and ethnic tension N.E. India with special reference to Manipur,' paper presented in the national seminar on Land problem and ethnic crisis in N.E. India, dated 27th to 28th July 2005, org. by MAKAIAS, Kolkata and Dept. of History, M.U.

Bharat Bhusan, Seminar paper on 'Ongoing peace process and negotiations in NE India—An analysis,' organised by NEPI at Guwahati on 7-9 September 2005.

Dolly Kikon, 'Carnival of Nationalism from the North-East Frontiers of India; interpreting Naga nationalism, questioning Indian autonomy and three suggestions for the Indo-Naga peace talks,' paper presented in the Second International Conference on Regional Autonomy and Ethnic Minorities, June 10-13, 2004 Uppsala, Sweden.

Seminar proceedings of 'Ethnicity and Politics,' org. by NRC at M.U. 16 Sept.2003.

M. Horam, 'The word Naga,' Unpublished Article.

YambemLaba, 'Kuki-Naga Conflict: An Insight,' Unpublished Manuscript, Imphal, 1995.

N. Khelchandra, 'Ching Amasung Tamgi Mari,' tr., Syncretic Relationship of Hills and Plains, Imphal 1998.

Seminar Proceedings on 'Land Reforms and Ethnic Crisis in North East India,' held on 27th and 28th July 2005 organised by MAKAIAS & History Department, MU.

vii) Ancient Manipuri Manuscripts
Chakpa Khunda Khunthok;
Tutenglon.

viii) Newspapers
The Imphal Free Press, 26 January 2005, Imphal.
The Freedom, 8, Dec.1993.
Resistance, 25th September 1979.
The Times of India, 8th may, 1985.
Nagaland Page, August 19, 2001.
The Statesman, October, 6, 1995.

ix) Private Reports and Souvenirs
A Brief Report of the UNC for the year 1995-1998, UNC Manipur, 1998.
A Report of NE Regional Seminar on Accords, peace process and prospects of civil society peace initiatives organized by NEPI, Guwahati, September 7, 2007,
Statement of the Report given by Camp Director Ito Tongbram in COFPAI (Committee for Peace and Integrity) campaign in 1995.
Expression of Freedom (1992-1994), Imphal. 12th December 1994.

x) Memorandums and Booklets
Aide-Memoir to the Prime Minister of India for Immediate creation of Kukiland, submitted by Kuki National Front (KNF) on 8 April 1998.
Memorandum submitted to Prime Minister of India on July 18, 1980 by ATSUM.

Index